Why Does Immigration Divide America?

Divide America?

Public Finance and Political Opposition to Open Borders

2007
M Renaissance Weekend

October 5–7, 2007

The Breakers
Palm Beach, Florida

Why Does Immigration Divide America?

Public Finance and Political Opposition to Open Borders

by Gordon H. Hanson

Washington, DC
August 2005

Gordon H. Hanson is a professor of economics in the Graduate School of International Relations and Pacific Studies and the Department of Economics at the University of California, San Diego (UCSD). He is also a research associate at the National Bureau of Economic Research and coeditor of the *Journal of Development Economics*. Before joining UCSD, he served on the faculties of the University of Michigan and the University of Texas. He is the author of over 50 academic research publications on the economic consequences of immigration, international trade and investment, and other aspects of globalization. His most recent book is *Immigration Policy and the Welfare System* (Oxford University Press, 2002).

**INSTITUTE FOR
INTERNATIONAL ECONOMICS**
1750 Massachusetts Avenue, NW
Washington, DC 20036-1903
(202) 328-9000   FAX: (202) 659-3225
www.iie.com

C. Fred Bergsten, *Director*
Valerie Norville, *Director of Publications
and Web Development*
Edward Tureen, *Director of Marketing*

Typesetting by BMWW
Printing by Kirby Lithographic Company, Inc.

Printed in the United States of America
07 06 05   5 4 3 2 1

Library of Congress Cataloging-in-Publication Data

Hanson, Gordon H. (Gordon Howard)
    Why does immigration divide America? : public finance and political opposition to open borders / Gordon Hanson.
        p. cm.
    September 2005.
    Includes bibliographical references and index.
        ISBN 0-88132-400-0 (alk. paper)
        1. United States—Emigration and immigration—Economic aspects.   2. United States—Emigration and immigration—Government policy.   3. Immigrants—Services for—United States—Finance.
    4. Illegal aliens—Services for—United States—Finance.   I. Institute for International Economics (U.S.)   II. Title.

JV6471.H36 2005
325.73—dc22   2005018633

Contents

Preface

During the 20 years since the last major reform of US immigration policy, illegal immigration has increased, wages of low-skilled US workers have fallen, and the short-run fiscal costs of immigration have grown. Yet there is no consensus on what ought to be done, even as added interest in national security has heightened the concern about what to do about the 10 million illegal immigrants living in the country.

Immigration, like other consequences of globalization such as trade or investment, has important effects on the distribution of income. Understanding these consequences and how they contribute to immigration policy are thus an important area of analysis for the Institute.

Gordon Hanson's study of the interplay of immigration policy, US labor markets, and the fiscal impact on US states of providing public services to immigrants is a key component of the Institute's large body of work examining the costs and benefits of globalization. Our other globalization studies include Lori Kletzer's *Job Loss from Imports: Measuring the Costs* (2001), J. David Richardson and Howard Lewis's *Why Global Commitment Really Matters!* (2001), Robert Baldwin's *The Decline of US Labor Unions and the Role of Trade* (2003), Kenneth Scheve and Matthew Slaughter's *Globalization and the Perceptions of American Workers* (2001), and J. David Richardson's forthcoming capstone volume, *Global Forces, American Faces: US Economic Globalization at the Grass Roots*. The first Institute study dealing specifically with migration, *Trade and Migration: NAFTA and Agriculture* by Philip Martin (1993), was published just before the North American Free Trade Agreement (NAFTA) came into effect and examined the likely impact of NAFTA on migration.

The Institute for International Economics is a private, nonprofit institution for the study and discussion of international economic policy. Its purpose is to analyze important issues in that area and to develop and communicate practical new approaches for dealing with them. The Institute is completely nonpartisan.

The Institute is funded by a highly diversified group of philanthropic foundations, private corporations, and interested individuals. Major institutional grants are now being received from the William M. Keck, Jr. Foundation and the Starr Foundation. About 33 percent of the Institute's resources in our latest fiscal year were provided by contributors outside the United States, including about 16 percent from Japan. A generous grant from the Andrew W. Mellon Foundation supported this and our other work on globalization.

The Institute's Board of Directors bears overall responsibilities for the Institute and gives general guidance and approval to its research program, including the identification of topics that are likely to become important over the medium run (one to three years) and that should be addressed by the Institute. The director, working closely with the staff and outside Advisory Committee, is responsible for the development of particular projects and makes the final decision to publish an individual study.

The Institute hopes that its studies and other activities will contribute to building a stronger foundation for international economic policy around the world. We invite readers of these publications to let us know how they think we can best accomplish this objective.

C. FRED BERGSTEN
Director
August 2005

Executive Summary

In this study, the author considers the interplay between public finance and US immigration policy. Immigration is making the US population larger and more ethnically diverse and the US labor force more abundant in low-skilled labor. One consequence of these changes has been lower wages for low-skilled US workers. More generally, the benefits and costs of immigration appear to be distributed quite unevenly. Capital owners, landowners, and employers capture most of the benefits associated with immigration, which they enjoy in the form of higher factor returns. Taxpayers in high-immigration US states shoulder most of immigration's fiscal costs, which they bear in the form of higher taxes that go to pay for public services used by immigrant households. On net, the economic impact of immigration on the United States is small. However, small net changes in national income mask potentially large changes in the distribution of income. These distributional changes appear to be an important ingredient in how individuals form opinions about immigration policy.

Survey data suggest that individuals are more opposed to immigration if they (1) are more exposed to immigration's labor-market consequences, as are low-income workers living in states with large immigrant populations, or (2) are more exposed to immigration's public finance consequences, as are high-income workers living in states with high immigrant uptake of public assistance. Policies that have reduced the fiscal costs of immigration, such as welfare reform in the 1990s, appear to have softened political opposition to immigration. Generating greater political support for open immigration policies would require reducing immigration's adverse effects on the labor-market earnings of and fiscal burdens on US residents.

Currently, there is political gridlock in the United States regarding immigration policy. This gridlock makes it difficult to address pressing issues related to illegal immigration, such as what to do about the 10 million illegal immigrants living in the United States, and national security, such as how to get immigration authorities and intelligence agencies to coordinate meaningfully with each other.

One strategy for reforming US immigration policy would be to change the skill composition of those admitted. By shifting to a system that favors high-skilled immigrants, the United States would attract individuals with high income potential. A skills-based immigration policy would help raise the wages of low-skilled workers and reduce the fiscal burden on taxpayers. However, it would have the disadvantage of having its effects on US labor markets blunted by other aspects of globalization. An alternative (but not mutually exclusive) strategy would be to expand temporary immigration programs and to phase in immigrant access to public benefits more slowly over time. A rights-based immigration policy would help alleviate the negative fiscal consequences of immigration and free immigration policy to be used for meeting US labor needs or achieving other objectives. To be effective, any change in immigration policy must address enforcement against illegal immigration.

Acknowledgments

I thank C. Fred Bergsten, Richard Cooper, Ken Scheve, Matt Slaughter, and seminar participants at the Council on Foreign Relations, Columbia University; the Institute for International Economics; the University of California, San Diego; and the University of Oregon for helpful comments. Jeff Lin and Sergio Khwanang provided excellent research assistance.

Introduction

Immigration is an issue capable of dividing like-minded people. Even groups whose members tend to agree on political issues—liberals, conservatives, isolationists, internationalists, environmentalists, free marketers—rarely share uniform opinions on US immigration policy. Neither major political party is unified in its position on the degree to which US borders should be open to foreign citizens.

Among Republicans, the business lobby persistently advocates for access to foreign labor. Emphasizing the economic benefits of immigration, the National Association of Manufacturers argues that "foreign nationals have made enormous contributions to US companies, our economy and society as a whole. To continue our economic and technological preeminence, we need to ensure that we have access to the talent we need to lead and compete" (www.nam.org). But many conservative groups oppose immigration on the grounds that it expands the welfare state, dilutes American culture, and threatens national security.[1] This split within the party manifested itself most recently in response to President Bush's 2004 pro-

---

1. According to Representative Tom Tancredo (R-CO), a leading congressional opponent of immigration, "There are 9 to 11 million illegal aliens living amongst us right now, who have never had a criminal background check and have never been screened through any terrorism databases. Yet the political leadership of this country seems to think that attacking terrorism overseas will allow us to ignore the invitation our open borders present to those who wish to strike us at home" (www.house.gov/tancredo/Immigration). Former Republican presidential candidate Pat Buchanan adds, "If America is to survive as 'one nation,' we must take an immigration 'time out' to mend the melting pot. . . . The enemy is already inside the gates. How many others among our 11 million 'undocumented' immigrants are ready to carry out truck bombings, assassinations, sabotage, skyjackings?" (www.issues2000.org/)

posal to grant illegal immigrants temporary legal status as guest workers, an initiative supported by business interests. The sharpest criticism of the plan came from lawmakers in Bush's own party. "Our offices have been inundated with calls from dismayed constituents expressing vehement opposition to the Administration's proposal," reported a letter from two dozen congressional Republicans. "Respect for the rule of law is a core conservative value. . . . We cannot continue to allow our immigration laws to be violated and ignored. . . . Illegal aliens are by definition criminals."[2]

Democrats are no more united. Union leaders have joined forces with Latino groups in support of permanent legal immigration and an amnesty for illegal immigrants.[3] But this stance runs counter to the opinions of many rank-and-file union members, who tend to favor closed borders (Scheve and Slaughter 2001a). Environmentalists are also split on immigration, due to its effects on US population growth. In 2004, an anti-immigration bloc attempted to gain control of the Sierra Club's board. The move failed, but the issue remains a source of conflict within the environmental movement.[4]

Such internecine disputes over immigration mirror differences of opinion in the electorate as a whole. When asked recently about immigrants' contributions to US society, over two-thirds of survey respondents acknowledged positive contributions (Scheve and Slaughter 2001b). But when asked what level of immigration they considered desirable, nearly half favored reducing the number of those admitted. The public thus appears to be roughly divided between those who favor scaling down immigration and those who support maintaining it at current levels. Americans appear to believe that immigration offers a range of potential benefits to the nation but simultaneously to worry about the associated costs of admitting large numbers of foreigners.

One result of divisiveness is inaction. Despite apparent agreement across the political spectrum that US immigration policy is in need of repair, the likelihood of serious reform appears slight. Current policy is widely faulted for failing to enforce at US borders and leaving large num-

---

2. Susan Jones, "Republican Lawmakers Won't Back Bush on Immigration," CNSNews.com, January 26, 2004. See also Christopher Wills, "Immigration, Bush Proposal Divides Republican Candidates," AP Wire, February 1, 2004, and Valerie Richardson, "Republicans Warn Bush on Immigration Policy," *Washington Times*, January 28, 2004.

3. The AFL-CIO endorses granting legal status to illegal immigrants but opposes guest-worker programs that provide immigrants anything less than full labor rights, www.aflcio.org/. This position is similar to that of the National Council of La Raza, www.nclr.org, whose president praised the AFL-CIO's decision to support an amnesty: "This policy change makes the full labor movement a partner in the immigrants' rights movement; we welcome their strong defense of immigrant workers. We applaud organized labor for taking this wise and courageous action."

4. See Juliet Eilperin, "Immigration Issue Sparks Battle at Sierra Club," *Washington Post*, March 22, 2004, A02.

bers of individuals in legal limbo. The US Census Bureau calculates that 300,000 to 500,000 net new illegal immigrants enter the United States each year (Costanzo et al. 2001). In 2004, the illegal population was estimated at 10.3 million, up from 3.8 million in 1990 (Passel 2005). In the aftermath of the 2001 terrorist attacks, the security of US borders has assumed renewed urgency. Yet border enforcement remains ineffective and the government still lacks the ability to track temporary legal immigrants.[5]

Few politicians or voters would endorse such high levels of illegal immigration or inadequate border controls. These outcomes appear to result from accommodation of opposing interests. Business lobbies for freer immigration but is countered by a diverse coalition that opposes open borders. The result is a system in which the government restricts the level of permanent legal immigration but allows less-visible types of immigration to adjust by changing the number of temporary work visas and the intensity with which it discourages illegal entry. Business gets access to foreign labor, but a third or more of these workers are illegal and many others are subject to the constraints of temporary immigration status. Illegality exposes US companies to legal risks and uncertainty about the labor supply and denies immigrants legal protections, ease of movement between jobs, and incentives to acquire skills and improve their communities.

Sources of Political Opposition to Immigration

Like international trade, foreign investment, and other aspects of globalization, immigration changes the distribution of income within a country. In the United States, a disproportionate number of immigrants have low skill levels: 33 percent of all foreign-born adults (both legal and illegal immigrants) had less than 12 years of education in 2003, compared with only 13 percent of native-born adults. By increasing the relative supply of low-skilled labor, immigration puts downward pressure on the wages of low-skilled native-born workers. George Borjas (2003) finds that between 1980 and 2000 immigration had the largest effect on the low-skilled, reducing the wages of native-born high-school dropouts by 9 percent.[6] The expanding supply and declining wages of low-skilled labor benefit labor-intensive industries, such as agriculture and apparel. Given these labor-market repercussions, we would expect low-skilled workers to be among

---

5. See Camarota (2002). In 2004 the US government announced that a contract had been awarded to the firm Accenture to develop a system to manage US borders and monitor entry and exit by foreigners, www.dhs.gov/dhspublic/index.jsp.

6. Many early studies of the labor-market consequences of immigration found that its wage impacts were small (Borjas 1999b). Recent studies find, however, that immigration depresses wages for the native workers most likely to substitute for immigrant labor (Borjas, Freeman, and Katz 1997; Borjas 2003).

those most opposed to immigration. In public-opinion surveys on immigration policy, Kenneth Scheve and Matthew Slaughter (2001b) found that opposition to immigration is indeed higher among the less educated, mirroring their skepticism about globalization in general.[7]

It does not appear, however, that labor-market effects alone can explain the current political divide on immigration. Adversely affected workers account for a relatively small share of the US electorate, both because the number of high-school dropouts is small and because they are relatively unlikely to vote. Clearly, there are other sources of opposition to immigration besides its consequences for labor markets. Among its myriad other effects, immigration alters public finances and politics at the local and national levels. Immigrants pay taxes, use public services, and, after naturalization, vote.

Concern that admitting low-skilled foreigners raises the net tax burden on US natives contributes to opposition to immigration. Low-skilled immigrants tend to earn relatively low wages, to contribute relatively little in taxes, and to enroll in government entitlement programs with relatively high frequency. There is abundant evidence that immigrants make greater use of welfare programs than do natives (Borjas and Hilton 1996; Borjas 1999a; Fix and Passel 2002). This pattern has persisted even after welfare reform in 1996 restricted immigrants' access to many government benefits (Zimmerman and Tumlin 1999; Fix and Passel 2002). In states with large immigrant populations, such as California, immigration appears to increase net burdens on native taxpayers substantially (Smith and Edmonston 1997).

This essay will examine the interplay between public finance and immigration policy.[8] Immigration affects the incomes of natives and earlier immigrants through its impacts on labor markets and on government taxes and transfers. By increasing the relative supply of low-skilled labor, immigration clearly tends to lower the pre-tax income of low-skilled labor relative to that of high-skilled labor. These labor-market outcomes help create opposition to immigration among the less-skilled. But immigration also affects after-tax income. If immigrants have access to public assistance, public education, and other public services, and if their contributions to tax revenues are insufficient to pay for their use of these services, governments will have to raise taxes on others, reduce services to others, and/or borrow from future generations. Any of these actions is likely to be unpopular, creating the potential for political action against immigration by individuals who expect to bear its costs.

---

7. See Rodrik (1997, 1998), Scheve and Slaughter (2001a, 2001b, 2001c, 2004), O'Rourke and Sinnott (2001, 2003), Mayda and Rodrik (2002), Hainmueller and Hiscox (2004), and Mayda (2004).

8. I will draw heavily on the analysis and results of Hanson, Scheve, and Slaughter (2005).

The substantial variation in the tax structures and spending policies of US states helps shape the politics of immigration. California and New York, for instance, impose high state income taxes and provide generous public benefits, while Florida and Texas have no state income tax and provide markedly less generous benefits. States also vary in the sizes of their immigrant populations. A handful of states—California, Florida, Illinois, New Jersey, New York, and Texas—have for several decades served as gateways for immigrants (Borjas 1999a). Most new immigrants settle in one or another of these states, disproportionately exposing their residents to the economic consequences of immigration. Recently settlement patterns have begun to change, exposing new regions to the direct effects of immigration. Since the 1990s, the Mountain, Southern, and Plains states—including, notably, Arizona, Colorado, Georgia, Nevada, and North Carolina—have begun to attract large numbers of immigrants (Passel and Zimmerman 2001; Card and Lewis 2005). Interaction between local tax and spending policies and the size of the local immigrant population determines who is subject to the costs and benefits of immigration, affecting which voters will favor immigration and which will not.

In the absence of distortionary tax and spending policies, economic theory suggests that low-skilled immigration would be supported by educated, high-skilled workers and opposed by less-educated, low-skilled workers. The available evidence is consistent with this prediction (see note 8). Theory also suggests that the positive correlation between skill and support for immigration would be strongest in states without generous welfare programs, where the labor-market effects of immigration are likely to outweigh the public-finance effects. In states whose public assistance to immigrants is more generous, the consequences of immigration for public finances are likely to be more influential politically. If such benefits are financed by progressive income taxes, as in California and New York, high-skilled, high-income individuals—who are most exposed to the fiscal burden associated with immigration—may join the low-skilled in opposing open borders.

A Tale of Two Governors

To understand better how public finance affects the politics of immigration, consider the recent histories of California and Texas. In the mid-1990s, both states had fiscally conservative governors who were rising stars in the Republican Party. Pete Wilson, elected in 1990, and George Bush, elected in 1994, were being touted as potential candidates for president; both had a great deal on the line politically.

Both governors faced difficult fiscal environments. California, battered by the post–Cold War decline in defense spending, experienced a severe recession in 1990–91 that left the state short on tax revenues. Wilson's battle with the state legislature over cuts in spending led to a two-month suspension of government payments. Texas bore the brunt of the savings-and-loan crisis in the late 1980s and sharp fluctuations in oil prices in the late 1980s and early 1990s. Meanwhile both states were absorbing much of the national surge in immigration. During the 1990s, as the foreign-born share of the US population grew from 8 percent to 11 percent, fully 37 percent of immigrants chose to reside in one of those two states (compared to only 17 percent of the native-born population).

Initially, Bush and Wilson appeared very similar politically. Both were unabashed free traders, and both strongly supported the North American Free Trade Agreement. When it came to immigration, however, they took very different approaches. Wilson made restrictions on public benefits for immigrants the centerpiece of his strategy to control spending in California. Most memorably, he backed Proposition 187, a ballot measure to deny public services to illegal immigrants.[9] Bush embraced Texas's immigrant population and courted Latino voters, even campaigning in Spanish.[10] He distanced himself from Proposition 187 and declared that he would not support such a measure in Texas.[11] In his 1998 gubernatorial bid, Bush won 49 percent of the Latino vote (and 69 percent of the total vote), the strongest showing ever among Texas Hispanics by a Republican in a statewide electoral race.[12]

History has already rendered its verdict on these strategies: Bush became president, and Wilson's success was short-lived. He did manage to get Proposition 187 passed, with the support of 59 percent of California voters. Subsequent political backlash against the measure, however, led to successful court challenges and inspired the Latino community and other pro-immigrant groups to organize in opposition to Wilson and the state Republican Party ("Nothing but Gravel in Their Pan," *The Economist*, March 7, 2002). The legacy of Proposition 187 appeared to contribute to the party's poor showing in statewide elections in 1998 and to Wilson's failed 2000 presidential campaign.

The experiences of California and Texas demonstrate how local tax and spending policies can influence the politics of immigration. In California, with its progressive income taxes and generous public benefits, high-income voters—an important constituency within the Republican Party—saw immigration as increasing their tax burden. These individuals, along-

---

9. Julie Marquis, "Wilson Blames Ills on Illegal Immigrants," *Los Angeles Times*, October 17, 1994, B1.

10. R. G. Ratcliffe, "Bush Ads Aim for Big Share of Hispanic Vote; Governor Speaks Spanish in Radio Spots," *Houston Chronicle*, August 15, 1998, A33.

11. Juan Palomo, "The Cool Headed Governor," *Hispanic Business*, December 1995, 12–16.

12. Ken Herman, "Bush Proves Ethnic Bona Fides," *Atlanta Journal and Constitution*, November 13, 1998, 4C.

The four chapters that follow develop my argument about the interaction between local public finance and preferences on immigration policy. Chapter 2 discusses current immigration policy using recent data from the Current Population Survey (CPS) to describe the evolution of US immigration trends. I will also review evidence on the labor-market consequences of immigration.

Chapter 3 examines immigrants' uptake of public benefits and the implied fiscal burden on native taxpayers. Variation in the size and composition of immigrant populations across US states suggests that immigrant demands for public services also vary by state. Furthermore, cross-state differences in the generosity of public benefits were made more extreme by federal welfare reform in 1996, which gave states discretion about which benefits to offer and whether to give immigrants access to those benefits. Among states whose immigrant populations are similar in size, those with more generous welfare programs in effect require each native household to pay for the benefits used by a greater number of immigrant households. States with generous benefits also tend to be those with progressive tax structures; thus higher-income households in these states are likely to shoulder a disproportionate share of the fiscal burden associated with providing public services to immigrants.

Chapters 2 and 3 suggest that the US residents most adversely affected by immigration will be low-wage workers, especially those in high-immigration states, and high-wage workers in high-immigration states with high immigrant uptake of welfare benefits. Chapter 4 uses data from National Election Studies surveys to examine whether opposition to immigration is stronger among individuals who expect to experience increases in labor-market competition or in net tax payments as a result of immigration. Consistent with previous studies, I find that opposition to immigration is stronger among the less educated, the group most exposed to the labor-market consequences of immigration. Building on the results of Hanson, Scheve, and Slaughter (2005), I also find the opposition of the low-skilled to be stronger in states with larger immigrant populations, where we expect the wage effects of immigration to be strongest. Among the highly educated, opposition to immigration is more intense in states where immigrants make greater use of means-tested entitlement programs. What appears decisive for this group is not residence in a high-immigration state per se, but residence in a high-immigration state characterized by high immigrant uptake of public assistance and other public benefits.

Chapter 4 suggests several potential strategies to defuse tensions over immigration and to move toward meaningful reform of US immigration policies. One such strategy is to alter the mix of immigrants admitted in favor of the high-skilled; this shift would reduce immigrant demand for public benefits and raise immigrant contributions to tax revenues. Another is to restructure immigrants' rights of access to public benefits, which would reduce immigrant draws on public expenditure.

In chapter 5, I discuss proposals for reforming US immigration policy. A shift toward skills-based immigration, as proposed by Borjas (1999a) and Huntington (2004), would eliminate the benefits that US consumers and employers derive from low-skilled immigration. It would also fail to confront the central question for US immigration policy: how to manage migrant inflows from Mexico. The impact on US wages of any shift from low-skilled to high-skilled immigration might also be partly offset by increased imports from, and US investment in, low-wage countries. Phasing in immigrant access to public benefits more slowly over time is a potentially more attractive and politically palatable approach to immigration reform. It would also create a framework in which policymakers could address Mexican immigration.

To be effective, any change in immigration policy must address illegal immigration. Enforcement at US borders, where immigration authorities currently devote most of their efforts, is ineffective. Despite massive increases in spending on border enforcement since the early 1990s, the inflow of illegal immigrants has not slowed. An alternative approach is to change the focus of enforcement to the hiring of illegal immigrants. Mandating information-sharing among immigration authorities, the Social Security Administration, and the Internal Revenue Service (via either a national identity card or electronic tracking of immigrants' visa status) would permit employers to verify instantly whether or not a potential employee is a legal immigrant. Such an approach could expand the capacity of immigration authorities to enforce against illegal immigration at workplaces in a manner that is effective, unobtrusive, and humane. The obtrusiveness of current efforts at enforcement in the US interior accounts in part for its political unpopularity.

During the 2004 presidential campaign, both candidates invoked immigration policy as an important topic deserving of attention. Both were predictably vague, however, about the best way to go about policy reform. The building consensus that US immigration policy is broken creates a political opening to address the issue. Continued inaction would be costly. Among other consequences, it would allow a large and growing segment of the US labor force to remain in a legal grey area, lacking the protections afforded by the law. Creating a strategy to reform immigration policy requires understanding, first, the economic consequences of immigration and, second, how these consequences shape public views on the number of foreigners who should be admitted to the United States.

2

US Immigration Policy and Recent Immigration Trends

Immigration to the United States has been on the rise since the late 1960s. After five decades of decline, the share of immigrants in the US population grew from 5 percent in 1970 to 12 percent in 2003 (see figure 2.1). The increasing presence of the foreign-born is attributable to high levels of legal and illegal immigration, both of which reflect recent changes in immigration policy. The influx of immigrants includes large numbers of Asians and Latin Americans, whose presence is altering the ethnic composition of the US population and the educational composition of the labor force.

Overview of US Immigration Policy

Immigration policy governs the admission of legal permanent and temporary immigrants and enforcement policies that affect the inflow of illegal immigrants. In addition to setting the level of immigration and criteria for admitting immigrants, US policy also determines the rights conferred on different classes of immigrants.

Current policy on permanent legal immigration is based on a quota system established by the Hart-Celler Immigration Bill of 1965.[1] Hart-Celler revised restrictive quotas based on national origin, which had originated with the Immigration Act of 1924, and made family reunification a central

---

1. For histories of US immigration policy, see Tichenor (2002) and Daniels (2003).

Figure 2.1 Share of the foreign-born in the US population, 1900–2003

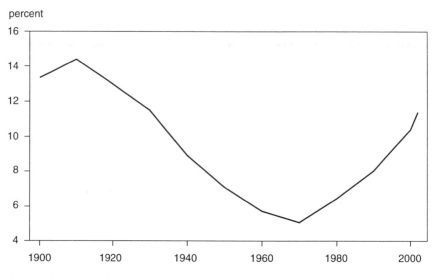

percent

Source: US Census of Population and Housing, various years.

feature of admission decisions.[2] The result was an increase in permanent legal immigration (see figure 2.2) and a change in the relative contribution of origin countries to US immigrant inflows (see table 2.1). Later changes in policy granted special status to refugees and asylees.[3] Under the present system, US Citizenship and Immigration Services (within the Department of Homeland Security) assigns applicants for permanent legal residence to one of seven categories, each subject to its own quota level.[4] The law guarantees admission to immediate family members of US citizens,

---

2. The 1924 law represented the first comprehensive restrictions on immigration to the United States, previously largely open to immigration from the rest of the world. The 1965 law amended the Immigration and Nationality Act of 1952, which had created skill-based categories but left unchanged the 1924 restrictions on national origin (Smith and Edmonston 1997).

3. The Refugee Act of 1980 created procedures for admission of refugees "of humanitarian concern," eliminating refugees and asylees as a category of the existing quota-preference system (DHS 2004).

4. In 2003, the Immigration and Naturalization Service (INS) was moved from the Department of Justice to the Department of Homeland Security (DHS). INS functions were distributed among three DHS agencies: Immigration-related services moved to US Citizenship and Immigration Services (USCIS), enforcement of immigration laws in the interior of the United States moved to US Immigration and Customs Enforcement (ICE), and enforcement of US borders, including the US Border Patrol, moved to the Bureau of Customs and Border Protection (CBP).

Figure 2.2 Permanent legal immigration to the United States, 1820–2000 (millions of people)

permanent legal immigration

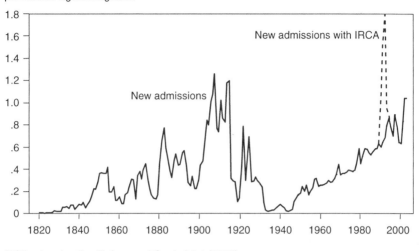

IRCA = Immigration Reform and Control Act (1986)

Source: US Department of Homeland Security, Office of Immigration Statistics, *2003 Yearbook of Immigration Statistics.*

who are exempt from entry quotas. Specific quotas apply to other family members of citizens, immediate family members of legal residents, individuals in special skill categories, and refugees and asylees facing persecution in their home countries.[5] Of the 705,827 permanent legal immigrants admitted in 2003, 70 percent gained entry as family members of US citizens or legal residents, 12 percent on the basis of employment preferences, 7 percent under the diversity program, 6 percent as refugees, and 5 percent in other categories (DHS 2004).

After five years as a permanent legal resident, an immigrant is eligible to apply for citizenship. Citizenship confers rights to vote and to draw on all government benefit programs for which an individual meets eligibility requirements. In 1996, as part of a comprehensive reform of federal welfare policies, Congress excluded noncitizen immigrants from many entitlement programs (Zimmerman and Tumlin 1999). A number of states have restored immigrants' access to certain programs, but the overall ef-

---

5. The Immigration Act of 1990 set a flexible cap for legal admissions at 675,000, of which 480,000 would be family-based, 140,000 would be employment-based, and 55,000 would be "diversity immigrants." The law also set temporary immigration at 65,000 in the H-1B program (high-skilled workers) and 66,000 in the H-2 program (short-term manual laborers), and created new categories for temporary admission of workers (O, P, Q, R). Subsequent legislation created categories for temporary immigration of professional workers from Canada and Mexico as part of the North American Free Trade Agreement (DHS 2004).

Table 2.1 Source countries of US immigrants, 2003

	Foreign-born population		Cohorts by arrival period			
	Level (thouands)	Percent of total	Pre-1970	1970–79	1980–89	1990–2003
			Number (thousands)			
All countries	34,612	100.0	4,759	4,983	8,213	16,657
			Percent of arrival-period cohort			
Region of birth						
Latin America	18,285	52.8	35.3	47.6	56.4	57.6
Asia	8,994	26.0	14.0	33.3	29.3	25.6
Europe	5,415	15.6	40.6	14.6	9.7	11.7
Other areas	1,918	5.5	10.1	4.5	4.6	5.0
Country of birth						
Mexico	10,237	29.6	16.0	26.4	30.1	34.1
Philippines	1,458	4.2	2.9	5.9	4.9	3.7
India	1,184	3.4	0.8	3.5	2.5	4.6
China	1,168	3.4	2.6	3.0	3.1	3.8
Germany	1,091	3.2	12.5	2.6	1.8	1.3
El Salvador	1,025	3.0	0.6	2.0	4.3	3.3
Cuba	1,005	2.9	7.9	2.9	2.2	1.9
Vietnam	947	2.7	0.5	4.5	3.4	2.5
South Korea	916	2.6	1.3	4.1	3.8	2.0
Canada	853	2.5	8.2	2.2	1.4	1.4
Dominican Republic	726	2.1	1.3	2.3	2.3	2.2

Source: March 2003 Current Population Survey.

fect of welfare reform was to impose a five-year waiting period before permanent immigrants have full access to public benefits (see table 2.2).

Additional legal immigrants are admitted on temporary work visas.[6] In 2003, the United States admitted 590,680 temporary workers and 135,933 immediate family members accompanying them (DHS 2004). The largest classes of immigrants on temporary work visas are high-skilled workers (H-1B), short-term manual laborers in agriculture (H-2A), and short-term manual laborers outside of agriculture (H-2B). To obtain a temporary work visa, an immigrant must be sponsored by a US employer. The H-1B visa was created in 1990 to permit foreigners with a college degree to work in the United States for a once-renewable three-year term. Most individuals on H-1B visas work in the electronics and software industries. Between 1998 and 2000, Congress raised the annual number of H-1B visas from 65,000 to 195,000; in 2003 it allowed the number of such visas to revert to 65,000. The H-2A visa, created by the Immigration Reform and Control Act of 1986, applies to seasonal laborers in agriculture. The H-2B visa applies

---

6. Large numbers of temporary entry visas are given to tourists, business travelers, and students, none of whom are eligible to work in the United States. The figures used here exclude these categories as well as temporary visas for foreign government officials (138,496 in 2003), and intracompany transferees, NAFTA workers, and their family members (168,580 in 2003) (DHS 2004).

Table 2.2 Current immigrant eligibility for welfare benefits

	SSI	Food stamps	Medicaid	TANF	Other federal means-tested benefits	State/local public benefits
Qualified immigrants arriving *before* August 23, 1996						
Legal permanent residents	Yes	No	State option	State option	State option	State option
Asylees, refugees[a]	Eligible for first 7 years	Eligible for first 5 years	Eligible for first 7 years	Eligible for first 5 years	Eligible for first 5 years	Eligible for first 5 years
Qualified immigrants arriving *after* August 23, 1996						
Legal permanent residents	No	No	Barred for first 5 years; then state option	Barred for first 5 years; then state option	Barred for first 5 years; then state option	State option
Asylees, refugees	Eligible for first 7 years	Eligible for first 5 years	Eligible for first 7 years	Eligible for first 5 years	Eligible for first 5 years	Eligible for first 5 years
Unqualified immigrants						
Illegal immigrants	No	No	Emergency services only	No	No[b]	No[c]
PRUCOL immigrants	No[d]	No	Emergency services only	No	No	No[c]

SSI = Supplemental Security Income
TANF = Temporary Assistance for Needy Families
PRUCOL = Persons residing under cover of law

a. This group includes Cuban and Haitian entrants, Amerasians, and aliens granted withholding of deportation.
b. States have the option to provide WIC to unqualified immigrants.
c. Selected programs are exempted, including short-term noncash relief, immunizations, testing and treatment for communicable diseases, and selected assistance from community programs.
d. Those immigrants already receiving SSI as of August 22, 1996, continued to be eligible until September 30, 1998.

Source: Boeri, Hanson, and McCormick (2002).

to hotel and restaurant workers, landscape workers, and other low-skilled workers in seasonal occupations. The bureaucratic procedure to obtain H-2A and H-2B visas is onerous, which appears to restrict their use. Between 2000 and 2003, the number of H-2A visas awarded annually ranged from 14,000 to 33,000; H-2B visas ranged from 51,000 to 103,000.

Though the United States does not explicitly set the level of illegal immigration, existing policy allows substantial numbers of illegal aliens to enter the country. In 2004, the illegal-immigrant population was estimated to be 10.3 million (Passel 2005).[7] During the 1990s, a net average of 300,000 to 500,000 new illegal immigrants entered the United States each year (Costanzo et al. 2001; INS 2003). Current policy on illegal immigration is based on the Immigration Reform and Control Act (IRCA) of 1986, which made it illegal to employ illegal aliens,[8] mandated monitoring of employers, and dramatically expanded border enforcement. Between 1980 and 2002, real expenditure on immigration enforcement increased 5.6-fold to $1.8 billion. IRCA also offered amnesty to illegal aliens who had resided in the United States since before 1982. As a result of IRCA, between 1988 and 1994 the United States granted permanent legal residence to 2.7 million individuals, 2 million of whom were Mexican nationals (Bureau of International Labor Affairs 1996) (see figure 2.2).[9]

Most illegal immigrants enter the United States by crossing the US-Mexico border or by overstaying temporary entry visas. The Border Patrol enforces against illegal immigration by policing the border and other points of entry and by seeking to prevent the smuggling and employment of illegal workers. In 2003, the Border Patrol apprehended 931,557 illegal aliens (89 percent of total apprehensions of illegal aliens by US immigration authorities).[10] Of those apprehended, 95 percent were Mexican nationals (DHS 2004). Most of the Border Patrol's activities are concentrated

---

7. This estimate of the illegal-immigrant population is based on the *residual foreign-born* as calculated from official government survey data. The number of residual foreign-born is derived by taking the enumerated immigrant population in the US Current Population Survey (or the US Census of Population and Housing) and subtracting new legal-immigrant admissions (less estimated departures and deaths among legal immigrants). The residual foreign-born population thus represents immigrants left over after accounting for net legal immigration. Since the CPS and the census appear to undercount the illegal-immigrant population by as much as 15 percent, the residual foreign-born calculation may underestimate the illegal-immigration population. See Bean et al. (2001), Costanzo et al. (2001), and INS (2001).

8. It had previously been illegal to "harbor" illegal aliens but not to employ them (Calavita 1992).

9. As a result of IRCA, net illegal immigration slowed during the late 1980s and early 1990s (since large numbers of illegal immigrants were becoming legal immigrants) but gross inflows of illegal immigrants appeared to continue at high levels (INS 2001).

10. Other apprehensions are by non–Border Patrol immigration authorities in the US interior. Apprehensions of illegal aliens overstate attempted illegal immigration in that a given individual may be captured by the Border Patrol multiple times in a given year.

in cities that border Mexico, such as San Diego, El Paso, and El Centro. This pattern has encouraged those attempting illegal entry to cross in the less populated—and more treacherous—desert and mountain regions of Arizona and eastern California.[11] In 2003, immigration authorities apprehended another 114,865 individuals (11 percent of total apprehensions) through interior enforcement activities. Very little border or interior enforcement occurs at US worksites. Of Border Patrol apprehensions in 2003, only 5,800 (0.6 percent of the total) occurred at US farms or other places of employment; the rest occurred at or near the US-Mexico border. Few employers face penalties for hiring illegal workers: Only 72 employers were convicted for employing illegal immigrants in 2003. Since 1986, fewer than two dozen employers have paid fines in excess of $75,000 for hiring illegal immigrants. These facts led the General Accounting Office to conclude in a recent report that, once in the United States, illegal immigrants appear to face little risk of apprehension or deportation (GAO 2002).

Illegal immigrants lack the rights granted to permanent and temporary legal immigrants, but they do enjoy some legal protections. The Supreme Court has ruled that the government may not deny public education or emergency medical services to foreign-born residents, even those in the country illegally. This ruling entitles illegal immigrants to send their children to public schools and to receive emergency medical care at hospitals. The US-born children of immigrants, whether their parents are legal or illegal, are eligible to receive welfare benefits designated for children, such as subsidized healthcare and school lunches. In practice, the Border Patrol rarely polices near schools, public-health facilities, churches, or other locales where apprehending illegal immigrants would be politically controversial. Combined with lack of enforcement at worksites, this pattern creates many public places where illegal immigrants may move about in relative freedom.

It is a common misperception that illegal immigrants do not contribute to tax revenues. Illegal immigrants pay sales taxes on their purchases and property taxes on dwellings they own or rent. Many also contribute to Social Security and to federal and state income taxes. Since passage of IRCA in 1986, employers are required to ask employees for proof of their employment eligibility. In response, many illegal immigrants present fake Social Security cards bearing invalid Social Security numbers. Most employers appear to treat illegal-immigrant employees as legal workers, withholding federal payroll taxes and income taxes from their paychecks. When paying payroll taxes on these workers, employers end up making contributions to invalid Social Security accounts.

The Social Security Administration holds contributions with invalid names or Social Security numbers in what is known as the Earnings Sus-

---

11. The end result of this policy has been an increase in deaths among illegal border crossers, from 50 a year in the early 1990s to 300–500 per year in the early 2000s (Cornelius 2001).

pense File. Since the late 1980s, when IRCA went into effect, inflows to the Earnings Suspense File have soared, from $7 billion in 1986 to $49 billion in 2000. As of 2003, the Earnings Suspense File contained $463 billion (Council of Economic Advisers 2005). The earliest contributions to the file date back to 1937, but the vast majority have accumulated since 1985 (Social Security Administration 2003). It seems highly unlikely that illegal immigrants who have contributed to invalid accounts will be able to draw on Social Security benefits in the future.[12] The holdings in the Earnings Suspense File, which initially amount to an interest-free loan from the contributors to the federal government, are eventually rolled into the Social Security Administration's general funds.

Many employers also withhold federal income taxes from the paychecks of illegal immigrants; the value of these contributions is hard to gauge. As a means of establishing a credit history, some self-employed illegal immigrants appear to pay income taxes voluntarily. This phenomenon may partially account for the rapid increase in the number of tax identification numbers issued by the Internal Revenue Service to individuals who are unable to obtain Social Security numbers. Between 1996 and 2003, the IRS gave out 6.8 million such tax ID numbers. By no means all of these tax IDs go to illegal immigrants; they are also issued to foreign students and researchers on temporary visas ("Illegal Aliens Paying Taxes," CBSNews .com, April 14, 2003). By the same token, it appears unlikely that all of these tax IDs could have gone to students and researchers, suggesting that the IRS has awarded tax IDs to many illegal immigrants.

Recent Trends in US Immigration

Immigration is making the US population larger and more ethnically diverse and the labor force more abundant in low-skilled labor. This section will use data from the Current Population Survey to review recent immigration trends (Current Population Survey, US Bureau of Labor Statistics, www.bls.census.gov/cps/cpsmain.htm). These data include both legal and illegal immigrants (see note 7), and among legal immigrants both permanent residents and those on longer-term temporary visas.

Predominance of Immigrants from Asia and Latin America

Of immigrants entering the United States between 1990 and 2003, 53 percent came from Latin America and 26 percent from Asia (see table 2.1). Mexico is the principal source country, accounting for 34 percent of all im-

---

12. At several junctures, Congress has contemplated action that would explicitly prohibit illegal immigrants from drawing on their contributions to Social Security. See Mark Stevenson, "Ban Sought on Benefits for Illegal Immigrants," Associated Press, August 31, 2004.

migrants arriving since 1990 and 30 percent of the total foreign-born population. The shift toward Asia and Latin America has diminished Europe's role. In 2003, 41 percent of immigrants who had entered the United States before 1970 came from Europe, compared with only 12 percent of those entering the country since 1990.

Estimates by the Census Bureau and academic demographers indicate that Asia and Latin America are even more dominant as source regions for illegal immigration.[13] In 2000, Asia and Latin America appear to have accounted for 75 percent of the illegal-immigrant population, up from 69 percent in 1990. Mexico is far and away the largest source of illegal immigrants, accounting for 57 percent of the illegal population in 2004 (Passel 2005). In 2000, the illegal share of the foreign-born population was 31 percent for all immigrants, 19 percent for immigrants from Asia, 36 percent for immigrants from Latin America, and 49 percent for immigrants from Mexico (Costanzo et al. 2001). Unsurprisingly, illegal immigration is correlated with economic conditions in Mexico, Central America, and other source regions. Attempted illegal immigration from Mexico surges following contractions in the Mexican economy, which tend to be particularly severe in the aftermath of the country's periodic currency crises. Border Patrol apprehensions increase 6 percent for every 10 percent decline in real wages in Mexico (Hanson and Spilimbergo 1999). Mexico's real wages fall sharply whenever the peso collapses (or unexpected inflation occurs). Thus Mexican economic crises typically produce large increases in the inflow of illegal immigrants from Mexico.

Overrepresentation at the Extremes of Skill Distribution

Immigrants are much more likely than US natives to have low levels of schooling. In 2003, 33 percent of immigrants 25 years and older had completed less than the equivalent of a high-school education, compared to only 13 percent of US natives (see figure 2.3). At the same time, immigrants are as likely as natives to be highly educated: 27 percent of each group had completed a bachelor's degree, and more immigrants than natives had completed an advanced degree. Where immigrants are strikingly underrepresented is among individuals with moderate schooling. Workers with a high-school diploma or some college account for 60 percent of native-born adults but only 41 percent of immigrants. The skill gap between natives and immigrants is one consequence of the shift in immigration away from Europe to Asia and Latin America, where prevailing levels of schooling are well below those in the United States (Borjas 1999a).

By increasing the supply of labor, immigration tends to drive down wages for US workers. Borjas (2003) estimates that between 1980 and 2000

---

13. See note 7 on methods used to estimate the illegal-immigrant population.

Figure 2.3 Educational attainment of immigrants and natives, March 2003

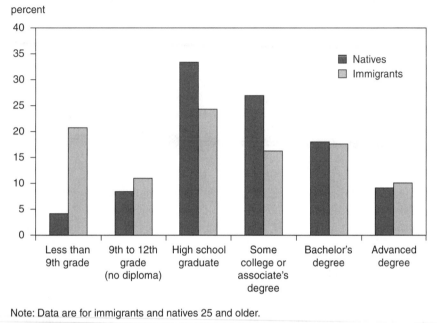

percent

Note: Data are for immigrants and natives 25 and older.

Source: March 2003 Current Population Survey.

immigration contributed to a decrease of 3 percent in the average wages of native workers. This estimate takes into account the total increase in the US labor force due to immigration, including both legal and illegal sources. Since immigration is concentrated among certain skill groups, its wage effects are most pronounced for low-skilled and high-skilled native workers; low-skilled workers suffered the largest wage declines. Borjas (2003) estimates that immigration lowered wages by 9 percent for native workers without a high-school degree, 3 percent for native high-school graduates, a negligible amount for natives with some college, and 5 percent for native college graduates.

Tendency Toward Low-Wage Occupations

Limited schooling and lack of legal status confine many immigrants to low-wage jobs. In 2003, 62 percent of natives but only 48 percent of immigrants were managers, professionals, or technical or administrative staff (see figure 2.4). Meanwhile only 25 percent of natives but 40 percent of immigrants worked in low-paying manual labor or agricultural occupations. Low-skilled immigrants are even more highly concentrated in

Figure 2.4   Occupational distribution of immigrants and natives, March 2003

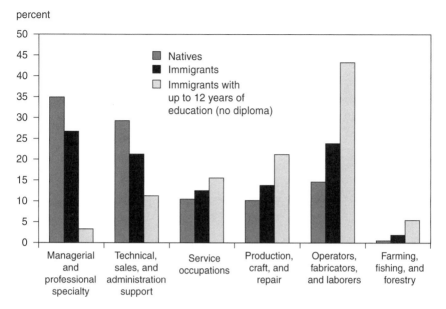

percent

Legend:
- Natives
- Immigrants
- Immigrants with up to 12 years of education (no diploma)

Categories (x-axis):
Managerial and professional specialty; Technical, sales, and administration support; Service occupations; Production, craft, and repair; Operators, fabricators, and laborers; Farming, fishing, and forestry

Source: March 2003 Current Population Survey.

low-paying occupations: 70 percent of immigrants with less than a high-school education work as manual laborers or in agriculture.

These differences in occupational outcomes are reflected in earnings. Among full-time year-round workers in 2003, 42 percent of all immigrants and 72 percent of those without a high-school diploma earned less than $25,000 a year, compared to only 25 percent of natives (see figure 2.5). Given native-immigrant differences in educational attainment, it is not surprising that immigrants are underrepresented in the middle of the earnings distribution. Fully 40 percent of native-born workers but only 28 percent of immigrants earned between $35,000 and $75,000 a year. Overall, the median earnings of native workers were 30 percent higher than those of immigrants.[14] Like the native-immigrant skill gap, the gap between native and immigrant earnings has grown over time (Borjas 1999b).

---

14. These differences in earnings do not control for differences in annual hours worked or for differences in age, education, and other characteristics between immigrants and natives. Using data from 1990 and controlling for differences in hours worked, Borjas (1999b) finds that natives earned 16 percent more than immigrants; controlling for age, education, and other observable characteristics as well, natives earned 10 percent more than immigrants. This pattern has changed markedly over time. In 1960, natives earned 4 percent less than immigrants (controlling for hours worked) and 1 percent less than immigrants (controlling for hours worked and other observable characteristics).

Figure 2.5   Yearly earnings distribution of immigrants and natives, March 2002

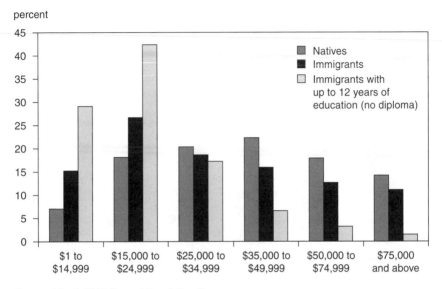

percent

Legend:
- Natives
- Immigrants
- Immigrants with up to 12 years of education (no diploma)

X-axis categories:
- $1 to $14,999
- $15,000 to $24,999
- $25,000 to $34,999
- $35,000 to $49,999
- $50,000 to $74,999
- $75,000 and above

Source: March 2003 Current Population Survey.

Illegality depresses the low earning potential of some immigrants. In an examination of illegal immigrants who attained legal status in the IRCA amnesty in the late 1980s and early 1990s, Sherrie Kossoudji and Deborah Cobb-Clark (2002) estimate that the penalty for illegal status in the 1980s was a wage 14 to 22 percent lower than that of legal workers. Much of this wage penalty appears to be due to the limited ability of illegal immigrants to move between jobs, which may suppress their bargaining power vis-à-vis employers. The low wages of illegal immigrants may be one reason that employers oppose increased enforcement against illegal immigration (Hanson and Spilimbergo 2001; Boeri, Hanson, and McCormick 2002).

Tendency to Settle in Specific Regions

On arrival in the United States, immigrants have tended in the past several decades to settle in the gateway states of California, Florida, Illinois, New Jersey, New York, and Texas. In 2003, these six states were home to 67 percent of immigrants but only 40 percent of the total population (see table 2.3). California alone is home to 28 percent of all immigrants but only 12 percent of all US residents. Within the gateway states, most immigrants live in a few large cities. In 2003, 46 percent of immigrants but only 17 percent of the native-born lived in just five metropolitan areas: Los Angeles, New York, San Francisco, Miami, and Chicago. Illegal im-

Table 2.3 Concentration of immigrants in six gateway US states

State	State share of total US population		State share of total US foreign-born population		Foreign-born share of total population	
	1994	2003	1994	2003	1994	2003
California	12.3	12.3	34.0	27.5	22.5	27.8
New York	7.0	6.7	11.7	11.7	13.6	21.0
Florida	5.4	5.7	9.3	8.8	13.9	18.6
Texas	7.0	7.5	9.0	10.4	10.4	16.8
New Jersey	3.1	3.0	4.5	4.4	12.0	17.6
Illinois	4.5	4.4	4.7	4.4	8.6	12.1
United States	—	—	—	—	8.2	12.1

Source: March 1994 and 2003 Current Population Surveys.

migrants are also concentrated regionally. In 2000, 68 percent of illegal immigrants lived in the six gateway states, 32 percent of them in California alone (INS 2001).

Immigrant settlement patterns have recently begun to change. The states with the fastest-growing immigrant populations in the 1990s were located in the Southeast (Georgia, North Carolina), Mountain West (Arizona, Colorado, Nevada), and Great Plains (Nebraska, Kansas) (see figure 2.6). These states also experienced high growth in native employment (see figure 2.7), which suggests that immigrants tend to move to regions where job growth is strong.[15] As chapter 3 will show, these states are not known for the generosity of their welfare benefits, further suggesting that their attractiveness to immigrants is driven by jobs and not by a desire for access to entitlement programs. The shift in population away from gateway states is even more noteworthy among the illegal foreign-born population. Between 1990 and 2000, the share of illegal immigrants residing outside the six gateway states increased from 20 to 32 percent (INS 2001).

The influx of low-skilled immigrants from Asia and Latin America is changing the US economy. Increasing the supply of low-skilled labor tends to drive down wages for low-skilled native workers, but also helps resuscitate industries that rely on manual labor. The arrival of immigrant workers appears to have helped meatpacking plants in the Great Plains, poultry-processing facilities in the South, and textile factories in the Southeast. Without immigrant labor, these industries might have shut down, with grave consequences for their regional economies. Immigrant

---

15. The correlation between the log change in the foreign-born share of the state population and the log change in state native employment from 1990 to 2000 is highly statistically significant, 0.53.

Figure 2.6 Immigrant share of state population, 1990 and 2000

2000 share/1990 share (log scale)

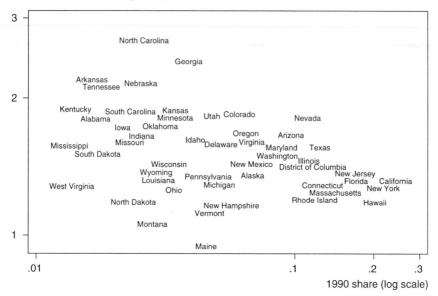

1990 share (log scale)

Figure 2.7 Growth in immigrant population and native employment rate, 1990 and 2000

immigrant share 2000/immigrant share 1990
(log scale)

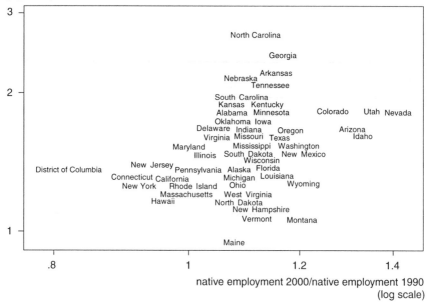

native employment 2000/native employment 1990
(log scale)

labor has also helped sustain the construction boom in the Southwest and Southeast that began in the 1990s. Economic theory suggests that the wage losses associated with immigration are more than offset by income gains to employers of immigrant labor. However, there is no reason to expect these offsetting gains to make immigration popular politically. By redistributing income away from manual labor and toward factory and farm owners, immigration creates winners and losers. Both groups are likely to appeal to their political representatives, either to reverse their losses or to secure their gains.

3

Immigrant Demands on Public Benefits

The predominance of the low-skilled among recent immigrants means that many new arrivals work in low-wage occupations and earn incomes toward the bottom of the earnings distribution. As low wage–earners, these immigrants are likely to pay little in taxes and to make large demands on public expenditures relative to other US residents. Compounding their demands on public services, immigrants also tend to have large families. These facts have raised concern that immigration causes a net drain on US public finances and increases the net fiscal burden on native taxpayers.

The tendency for immigrants to concentrate in certain geographic areas means that the public-finance consequences of immigration are likely to vary regionally. Residents of states with larger populations of low-skilled immigrants will naturally bear a larger share of the fiscal cost associated with immigration. In addition to regional disparities, states also vary in the generosity of the public benefits they provide. Residents of states that both attract immigrants and offer generous benefits are those most exposed to immigration's net fiscal burden.

Immigrant and Native Use of Welfare Programs

Public services take many forms, including public safety (fire and police protection), public spaces (parks and recreation facilities), education, healthcare, and public assistance (welfare). It is immigrants' access to public healthcare and public assistance that has proven most controversial. The Current Population Survey (CPS) presents information on individual participation in various types of social assistance in its Annual Demographic Files (the March Supplement). I will use CPS data for the 1994–2003 period to examine immigrant and native receipt of welfare benefits. Like the US Census of Population and Housing, the CPS includes both legal and illegal immigrants; among legal immigrants, it includes both permanent residents and those on temporary work and study visas.[1]

I classify individuals as members of households headed by a foreign-born or a native-born individual and then examine household members' usage of social assistance. Thus I count the US-born children of immigrants as members of immigrant-headed households as long as they reside with their parents or other foreign-born relatives. This approach in effect ascribes the welfare behavior of children to their parents. Households are natural groupings to examine; they are the units on which government agencies assess income taxes, property taxes, and other levies. When determining individual eligibility for means-tested benefit programs, it is typically the characteristics of the household that are taken into account (Zimmerman and Tumlin 1999). Following the academic literature, I classify a household as receiving welfare if any member received any type of social assistance, whether cash or in-kind benefits. I also examine participation by immigrant and native households in four specific entitlement programs: general assistance or Temporary Assistance for Needy Families (TANF), Supplemental Security Income (SSI), Medicaid, and food stamps.[2]

In 2002, immigrant-headed households were much more likely than native-headed households to participate in welfare programs (see table 3.1). Among immigrant households, 24.2 percent had at least one member who used some type of social assistance, compared to 14.9 percent of native households. Thus, 9.3 percent more immigrant than native households received public benefits. Since the early 1990s, academic researchers have consistently found immigrants more likely than natives to receive social assistance (Borjas and Hilton 1996; Borjas 1999a and 2002). Given that immigrants are relatively likely to earn low incomes and to live in poverty, this is hardly surprising. Participation in welfare programs is means-tested, and household income and size are the key determinants of eligibility.

---

1. As discussed in note 7 in Chapter 2, the census and the CPS are likely to undercount illegal immigrants. Most recent estimates of the undercount rate range from 5 percent to 15 percent.

2. The other noncash benefits on which the CPS collects data are energy assistance; housing assistance; school breakfasts and lunches; and Women, Infants, and Children (WIC). Prior to welfare reform in 1996, TANF was known as Aid to Families with Dependent Children (AFDC). SSI provides cash benefits to the disabled and to the elderly who lack other means of support.

Table 3.1 National trends in welfare participation rates
(percent of households receiving assistance)

Year		Some type of assistance	Some type of cash benefit	TANF or general assistance	SSI	Medicaid	Food stamps
1994	Native	15.3	7.7	4.5	3.9	13.3	8.4
	Immigrant	24.6	12.9	8.1	6.2	22.4	13.7
1995	Native	14.8	7.4	4.1	3.9	13.0	7.9
	Immigrant	24.7	12.7	7.8	6.2	22.6	12.7
1996	Native	15.1	7.3	3.8	4.2	13.3	7.8
	Immigrant	22.8	11.6	6.5	6.1	21.3	11.3
1997	Native	13.8	6.5	3.0	4.0	12.3	6.7
	Immigrant	21.0	10.0	5.0	5.8	19.4	10.0
1998	Native	13.2	5.8	2.5	3.8	11.9	5.8
	Immigrant	20.6	9.2	4.2	5.7	19.3	8.2
1999	Native	13.1	5.5	2.1	3.8	11.9	5.2
	Immigrant	20.0	8.5	3.5	5.6	18.9	7.3
2000	Native	13.5	5.1	1.8	3.7	12.4	5.1
	Immigrant	21.4	7.6	2.7	5.3	20.3	6.2
2001	Native	14.3	5.0	1.6	3.8	13.1	5.3
	Immigrant	23.4	7.2	2.6	5.1	22.5	6.3
2002	Native	14.9	4.9	1.6	3.6	13.6	5.5
	Immigrant	24.2	6.9	2.3	5.0	23.2	6.5

TANF = Temporary Assistance for Needy Families
SSI = Supplemental Security Income

Source: Current Population Survey, Annual Demographic Files, various years.

The nationwide immigrant-native differential in overall welfare use has fluctuated over time but does not show a consistent trend (see figure 3.1). In 1994, the share of households receiving any type of welfare was 24.6 percent for immigrants and 15.3 percent for natives, the same differential (9.3 percent) as in 2002. Between 1994 and 1999, both groups reduced their welfare use, natives by 2.2 percent (15.3 percent to 13.1 percent) and immigrants by 4.6 percent (24.6 percent to 20.0 percent). During the late 1990s, the immigrant-native differential in overall welfare use thus declined from 9.3 percent to 6.9 percent.

Initially, academic researchers attributed the 1990s-era decline in immigrants' welfare uptake to the reform of federal welfare programs undertaken by Congress in 1996 (Fix and Passel 2002; Borjas 2002). The reform mandated being employed as a precondition to receive benefits, limited lifetime use of certain benefits, gave states more discretion over program design, and excluded noncitizens from access to many benefits. Congress replaced state entitlements to open-ended federal funds with block grants, resulting in considerable state autonomy over individual eligibility criteria. States may decide whether or not to use their federal block grants to provide TANF, Medicaid, and other benefits to legal immigrants

Figure 3.1 Nationwide difference in immigrant and native welfare-participation rates, 1994–2002

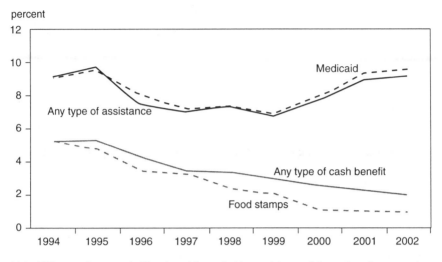

Note: Difference is percent of immigrant households receiving assistance less the percent of native households receiving assistance.

Source: Current Population Survey, Annual Demographic Files, various years.

who arrived before 1996 (see table 2.2). They may not use federal block grants to provide these benefits to legal noncitizen immigrants who arrived after 1996, but may use other state funds to create substitute programs.[3] States now vary considerably in the benefits they offer to immigrants (Zimmerman and Tumlin 1999) (see figure 3.2).

After five years of residence, immigrants may apply for citizenship, which guarantees access to public benefits for which they meet standard eligibility criteria. For new immigrants, this requirement in effect mandates a minimum five-year waiting period for access to most benefits. Denying noncitizens access to benefits thus raises the incentives to naturalize. Borjas (2002) finds that naturalization rates among immigrants have risen sharply since welfare reform, especially in California where naturalization offers relatively large gains in terms of access to public assistance.

The late 1990s were a difficult period in which to evaluate the effects of welfare reform. The United States had been enjoying a sustained economic expansion for several years. If the boom helped low-income workers more than other workers, immigrants may have enjoyed relatively large income gains, causing them to leave welfare rolls in relatively large numbers. The

---

3. Some states, including California and Texas, have chosen to provide some health services to illegal immigrants. Their motivation appears to be that it is more cost-effective to do so than for these individuals to use emergency medical services. See Clay Robison, "Senate approves care for illegal immigrants," *Houston Chronicle*, May 5, 2003, A19.

Figure 3.2 Availability of welfare benefits to immigrants by state, 1996–present

		Generosity of public assistance to all citizens			
		1	2	3	4
Public assistance availability to immigrants	4	Illinois	Missouri Nebraska	California Maine Maryland Massachusetts Rhode Island	Washington
	3	Florida	Oregon	Connecticut Minnesota New Jersey New York Pennsylvania Wisconsin	Hawaii
	2	Delaware District of Columbia Kentucky Montana Nevada North Carolina Tennessee Virginia Wyoming	Alaska Arizona Colorado Georgia Iowa Kansas New Mexico North Dakota Utah	Michigan	New Hampshire
	1	Alabama Arkansas Idaho Louisiana Mississippi Ohio Texas West Virginia	Indiana Oklahoma South Carolina South Dakota		

Note: Higher numbers indicate greater generosity of benefits to all citizens and greater availability of benefits to noncitizens.

Source: Zimmerman and Tumlin (1999).

early 2000s, which brought a recession and slow economic recovery, allow us to examine welfare use during a period of slow economic growth. From 1999 to 2002, use of social assistance increased by 4.2 percent for immigrants and 2.7 percent for natives. The larger increase in welfare use by immigrants erased the effects of the late 1990s and left the immigrant-native differential in overall welfare use in 2002 identical to that in 1994.

Does this pattern mean that welfare reform has not in fact affected the frequency with which immigrant households use social assistance? Though the immigrant-native differential in overall welfare use has not changed over time, the composition of benefits received by immigrants and natives has changed. In 1994, the share of households receiving some type of cash benefit (general assistance, AFDC, or SSI) was 5.2 percent greater among immigrants than among natives (see table 3.1 and figure 3.1). By 2002, this differential had fallen to 2.0 percent. Similarly, the differential between immigrant and native use of food stamps declined from 5.3 percent to 1.0 percent between 1994 and 2002. Medicaid is the only major category in which the immigrant-native welfare differential did not fall. (It actually increased, from 9.1 percent to 9.6 percent.) The share of immigrant households using all types of social assistance except Medicaid has declined, both in absolute terms and relative to natives. This finding suggests that welfare reform has had the intended effect of limiting immigrants' access to many types of public benefits. What appears to explain immigrants' continued access to Medicaid is that US-born children are eligible regardless of the citizenship of their parents. Many immigrant-headed households may have retained their access to Medicaid by virtue of having children who are US citizens.[4]

That many immigrant families have lost access to cash benefits but not to health benefits may reflect variation in the cost that voters ascribe to different types of public assistance. Native voters may be more willing to support immigrants' access to healthcare than to provide unconstrained cash payments to immigrants, especially when that healthcare is provided to children (who as US citizens may be the only members of many immigrant households eligible to use Medicaid).

Variation in Welfare Use by State

As we have seen, welfare reform granted the states discretion in setting eligibility requirements for noncitizens and in allocating funds for social assistance. Even before welfare reform, however, states varied in the generosity of the public benefits they offered. In the mid-1990s, the share of households receiving some type of public assistance ranged among natives from 4 percent in Nevada to 24 percent in Tennessee and among immigrants from 3 percent in Alabama to 37 percent in New Mexico (see figure 3.3a). After welfare reform, states also varied in the extent to which they granted noncitizens access to entitlement programs (see figure 3.3b). A recent study by the Urban Institute shows that the states that offer more expansive benefits also tend to make benefits more available to noncitizens (Zimmerman and Tumlin 1999). States situated in the upper-right corner of figure 3.2 (such as California, Massachusetts, New Jersey, and New York) offer relatively generous benefits and high availability to noncitizens; states

---

4. See Leighton Ku, Shawn Fremstad, and Mathew Broaddus, "Noncitizens' Use of Public Benefits Has Declined since 1996: Recent Report Paints Misleading Picture of Impact of Eligibility Restrictions on Immigrant Families," Center for Budget and Policy Priorities, www.cbpp.org/4-14-03wel.htm).

Figure 3.3 Share of native and immigrant households receiving public assistance

a. 1994–95

percent of immigrant households

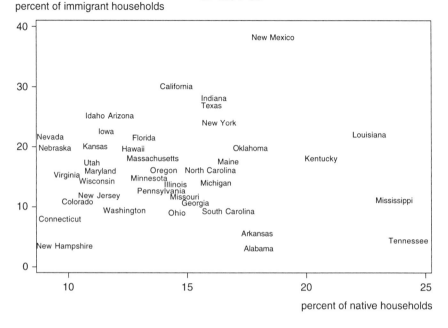

percent of native households

b. 2002–03

percent of immigrant households

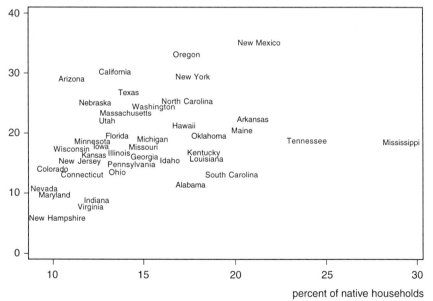

percent of native households

in the lower-left corner (such as Arizona, Colorado, Georgia, Nevada, North Carolina, and Texas) provide relatively stingy benefits and low availability to noncitizens. Few states are characterized by low generosity with high availability to noncitizens (upper-left corner) or by high generosity with low availability to noncitizens (lower-right corner).

Unsurprisingly, immigrant uptake of welfare is higher in the more generous states. Table 3.2 shows usage of social assistance by immigrant and native households in more and less generous states. (More generous states are defined as those that offer both generous benefits overall and high availability to noncitizens.) In 2002, the differential in immigrant welfare use between more-generous and less-generous states was 4.8 percent for any type of social assistance (25.5 percent to 20.7 percent), 4.9 percent for cash benefits (8.3 percent to 3.4 percent), and 5.3 percent for Medicaid (24.7 percent to 19.4 percent). Each of these differentials in welfare use is larger than the corresponding differential for native households.

Benefit programs are means-tested; thus the more low-income immigrants reside in a state, the more households will be eligible to receive welfare. Household income depends heavily on the education of the household head. Figure 3.4 shows a strong negative relationship between the average income of immigrant household heads in a given state and the fraction of those households whose head has less than a high-school education. Controlling for other observable characteristics, the difference in the likelihood that a household receives cash welfare benefits is 8 (4) percent between households headed by an immigrant with less than a high-school education and those headed by a college-educated (high-school-educated) immigrant.[5]

The interaction between state welfare policies and the size and characteristics of the immigrant population determines a state's total immigrant welfare usage. To gauge the potential fiscal burden represented by immigrant uptake of social assistance, figure 3.5 plots the ratio of immigrant households in a state receiving some type of welfare benefit to the number of native households. This ratio produces a crude metric for the number of immigrant households that each native household must support. In 2002–03 there were over 20 native households for each immigrant household on welfare in Texas, Florida, Nevada, and New Jersey, but 10 or fewer native households for each immigrant household on welfare in California and New York. All of these states have large immigrant populations. What distinguishes California and New York is that these states have large low-skilled immigrant populations and generous welfare policies. Native

---

5. These estimates are based on an ordinary least squares regression in which the dependent variable is a 0–1 indicator for whether an immigrant household receives some type of cash welfare benefit (general assistance, SSI) and the independent variables are the age, age squared, years of education, marital status, and year of entry into the United States of the household head; the size of the household; and state dummy variables. Data are from the 2000 United States Census of Population and Housing 5% Public Use Microsample.

Table 3.2 Native and immigrant welfare participation in more and less generous states, 1994–2002

Year	Natives		Immigrants	
	Less generous states	More generous states	Less generous states	More generous states
Welfare participation rates (percent of households receiving some type of assistance)				
1994	16.7	13.9	22.8	25.2
1995	15.8	13.7	22.9	25.2
1996	16.2	13.9	19.3	24.0
1997	14.7	12.9	17.1	22.4
1998	13.9	12.6	16.9	21.9
1999	13.6	12.6	15.5	21.5
2000	14.0	12.9	15.4	23.7
2001	15.2	13.4	18.5	25.3
2002	16.0	13.7	20.7	25.5
Cash program participation rates (percent of households receiving cash assistance)				
1994	7.7	7.6	8.2	14.3
1995	7.2	7.5	8.2	14.0
1996	7.0	7.6	7.4	13.1
1997	6.6	6.4	6.1	11.3
1998	5.7	6.0	5.6	10.5
1999	5.4	5.6	4.7	9.9
2000	5.1	5.1	3.4	9.1
2001	5.1	4.9	3.5	8.6
2002	4.9	4.9	3.4	8.3
Medicaid participation rates (percent of households receiving Medicaid)				
1994	14.1	12.4	18.6	23.6
1995	13.5	12.4	19.5	23.6
1996	14.0	12.6	17.2	22.7
1997	12.8	11.8	15.2	20.9
1998	12.2	11.6	15.4	20.7
1999	12.2	11.7	13.8	20.7
2000	12.5	12.2	14.0	22.6
2001	13.7	12.6	17.3	24.5
2002	14.5	12.8	19.4	24.7
Food stamp participation rates (percent of households receiving food stamps)				
1994	9.6	7.3	14.2	13.6
1995	8.6	7.1	13.1	12.6
1996	8.3	7.2	11.0	11.4
1997	7.3	6.0	9.2	10.3
1998	6.4	5.2	5.7	9.1
1999	5.8	4.6	6.2	7.7
2000	5.8	4.3	4.8	6.7
2001	6.2	4.3	5.3	6.7
2002	6.3	4.6	5.8	6.8

Source: Current Population Survey, Annual Demographic Files, various years.

Figure 3.4   Average immigrant household-head income and share of immigrant households headed by a high-school dropout, 2002–03

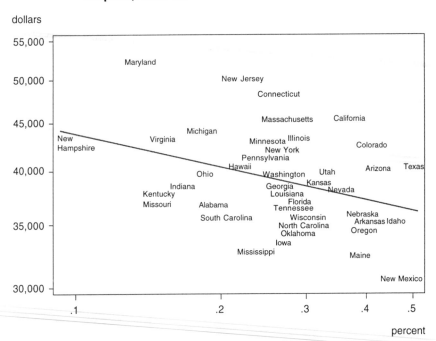

Note: The Y axis shows average earnings of immigrant household heads and the X axis shows percent of immigrant households headed by a high-school dropout.

taxpayers in California and New York are highly exposed to the fiscal costs associated with immigration; taxpayers in Texas, Florida, Nevada, and New Jersey appear likely to face a smaller burden. The next section will examine in more detail the costs of providing public services to immigrants.

The Costs and Benefits of Immigration

Immigration increases the incomes of US residents by allowing firms to utilize domestic resources more efficiently. These benefits, however, are not shared equally. Immigration redistributes income away from groups that compete with immigrants in the labor market. This redistribution is one source of political opposition to immigration. A second source of opposition arises from the costs that immigration imposes on native taxpayers. If immigrants receive more in government benefits than they pay in taxes, immigration imposes a net fiscal burden on US natives. To lower their fiscal burden, taxpayers may favor reducing immigration.

Figure 3.5 Immigrant households on welfare, 2002–03

immigrant households on welfare/native households

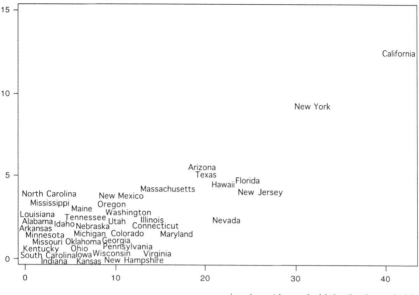

immigrant households/native households

Immigration generates benefits to a nation in the form of extra income to domestic factors of production, a phenomenon known to economists as *the immigration surplus*. By increasing the supply of labor in an economy, immigration raises the productivity of factors that are complementary to labor. For instance, a larger supply of low-skilled workers enables US capital, land, natural resources, and skilled labor to be exploited more efficiently. These gains in productivity generate income gains to owners of these factors. As we saw in chapter 2, an increase in the supply of labor also drives down wages for some US workers. To calculate the net change in national income associated with immigration, we can sum up the income changes associated with immigration for all domestic factors of production. Using a simple model of the US economy,[6] the immigration surplus takes a tractable form:

Immigration surplus as a percentage of GDP =
–0.5 * (percent change in wages due to immigration)
* (percent change in labor force due to immigration)
* (labor as a share of national income).

6. This model assumes one good and two factors of production. It is straightforward to extend this model to a more complicated environment.

Applying this formula to Borjas's data (2003) for the 1980–2000 period results in a crude calculation of the immigration surplus for the US economy in 2000:

$$0.5 * (3.2\%) * (11\%) * (0.70) = 0.12\%.$$

According to this formulation, immigration raises US GDP by slightly more than one-tenth of a percent, a very modest benefit.[7] The benefit would be larger if the wage change associated with immigration were larger, which would require either a higher level of immigration or a shift in the composition of immigrants toward individuals whose skills are in scarce supply.

In an economy free of distortions due to market failure or government intervention, there would be no costs associated with immigration. However, US tax and spending policies distort individual decisions about how much to work, how much to save, and how much to invest. Immigration of large numbers of low-skilled individuals may exacerbate these distortions by expanding the welfare system. If immigrants in the aggregate pay less in taxes than they receive in government benefits, immigration would generate a net fiscal burden on native taxpayers; that is, natives would in effect be making an income transfer to immigrants. Paying for this transfer would require some combination of tax increases on natives, reductions in government benefits to natives, and increased borrowing from future generations (by issuing government debt). The total impact of immigration on US residents is positive only if the immigration surplus exceeds the fiscal transfer to immigrants.

The National Research Council (NRC) recently conducted case studies of the fiscal impacts of immigration in New Jersey and California (Smith and Edmonston 1997). Both states have large immigrant populations, but their skill profiles and patterns of welfare usage differ. In 2002, the share of immigrant households headed by an individual without a high-school diploma was 37 percent in California but only 22 percent in New Jersey; the share of immigrant households receiving some type of social assistance was 30 percent in California but only 15 percent in New Jersey.

On the basis of federal, state, and local government expenditures and tax receipts, the NRC estimates that the short-run fiscal impact of immigration is negative in both New Jersey and California.[8] In New Jersey,

---

7. This estimate of the immigration surplus ignores many factors and should be treated with caution. More sophisticated estimates of the immigration surplus allow for labor of different skill types and varying effects of immigration on wages (see Borjas 1999b). Dynamic effects of immigration, such as increased innovation due to an inflow of new ideas or highly-skilled workers from abroad, are very hard to gauge. If they are important, static estimates of the immigration surplus will tend to understate immigration's true economic impact.

8. The study included all federal, state, and local government services and sources of tax revenue for which it was feasible to collect data. See Smith and Edmonston (1997) for details.

using data for 1989–90, immigrant households received an average net fiscal transfer from natives of $1,484, or 2 percent of average immigrant household income in the state.[9] This transfer amounted to an average net fiscal burden of $232 per native household, or 0.4 percent of average native household income. In California, using data for 1994–95, immigrant households received an average net fiscal transfer of $3,463, or 9 percent of average immigrant household income, which amounted to an average fiscal burden on native households of $1,178, or 2 percent of average native household income. In California, and to a lesser degree in New Jersey, the net fiscal transfers that native households make to immigrant households are large. The continuing increase in the immigrant population suggests that these transfers are likely to grow over time, raising the potential for political opposition to immigration from native taxpayers.

Natives' political response to making fiscal transfers to immigrants probably depends on the nature of the services that these transfers support. If transfers are seen as investments in immigrants or their children, via education or preventive healthcare, they may not provoke much opposition. The NRC estimates that K–12 education's share of total state and local government expenditures on services to immigrant households was 37 percent in California and 66 percent in New Jersey. Education's higher share in New Jersey expenditures reflects the state's low provision of other types of services relative to California. If native voters tend to approve of government expenditures on education, estimates of total net transfers to immigrants may overstate the fiscal impact that native voters perceive.

The NRC finds that two factors explain net fiscal transfers to immigrants: (1) immigrant households have more children, and thus make greater use of public education, and (2) immigrant households earn less, leading to greater use of welfare programs and lower tax contributions. Native taxpayers in California, with its less-skilled immigrant population and high immigrant uptake of welfare, make relatively large fiscal transfers to immigrant households. This pattern suggests that the fiscal costs of immigration are borne unevenly: States with poorer immigrant populations and more generous policies are likely to shoulder a much larger share of the fiscal burden associated with immigration. Further magnifying the distributional consequences of immigration, California and certain other high-immigration states have progressive tax systems in which high-income taxpayers pay a disproportionate share of taxes. Thus higher-income taxpayers in high-immigration states are likely to pay much of the fiscal cost of immigration.

The NRC's estimated fiscal transfers associated with immigration occur entirely at the state and local levels, where immigration has a decidedly negative impact on public finances. At the federal level, immigrants make

---

9. All figures drawn from the NRC study are in 1996 dollars.

a positive net fiscal contribution. This is the case because national defense accounts for a large fraction of the federal benefits that immigrants receive. As a public good, the cost of national defense is unaffected by immigration. Adding taxpayers through immigration, however, lowers the effective amount the federal government must charge native taxpayers to cover defense outlays.

For the nation as a whole, the NRC estimates that immigration imposes a short-run burden on the average native household of $166 to $226, or 0.20 percent to 0.25 percent of GDP in 1995. Comparing the average of these two estimates to the immigration surplus of 0.12 percent of GDP, a back-of-the-envelope calculation suggests that in the short run immigration reduces the aggregate income of US residents by about 0.1 percent of GDP. Turning from a short-run to a long-run estimate of the fiscal cost of immigration can change the results dramatically.[10] Under any scenario, however, the long-run fiscal impact of immigration on state and local governments is negative. Thus, in both the short run and the long run, state and local governments (and the taxpayers who support them) pick up much of the fiscal tab associated with immigration.

The benefits and costs of immigration appear to be distributed quite unevenly. Capital owners, landowners, and employers appear to capture most of the benefits associated with immigration in the form of higher factor returns. Taxpayers in high-immigration states are likely to shoulder most of immigration's fiscal costs in the form of higher taxes that go to pay for net fiscal transfers to immigrant households. On net, the economic impact of immigration on the United States appears to be small. However, small net changes in national income can mask large changes in the distribution of income. It is these distributional consequences that are likely to shape individual opinions on immigration policy.

---

10. The NRC estimates that the average immigrant admitted in 1990 would produce a net fiscal contribution of $80,000 over the next 300 years (in present-discounted-value terms). Looking ahead 300 years requires very strong assumptions about the future economic environment. The average immigrant's annual net fiscal contribution is negative for the first 25 years after arriving in the United States. The long-run estimate rests on the assumption that the federal government will eventually raise taxes to bring the federal budget into balance. If this does not happen, the long-run fiscal contribution of the average immigrant will be negative. See Borjas (1999a) for a discussion.

4

Public Preferences
on Immigration Policy

Changes in US policy have led to more immigration overall and from Asia and Latin America in particular. Since poor countries tend to have populations with low educational attainment, it comes as little surprise that a large fraction of recent immigrants arrive with relatively little schooling. The influx of immigrants appears to have depressed average wages in the United States, and the largest wage losses have been borne by low-skilled native workers.

Immigration also appears to affect native incomes through its impact on public finances. US immigration policy increases the population of individuals who demand public services, the population of taxpayers who contribute to public coffers, and the population eligible to gain citizenship and to vote. In the absence of immigration, the short-run net tax burden on native taxpayers in the nation as a whole would have been smaller; in high-immigration states like California, the burden would have been considerably smaller.

The distributive consequences of immigration are likely to affect public attitudes about immigration policy. Kenneth Scheve and Matthew Slaughter (2001a, 2001b, 2001c) have found that less-skilled workers are more likely than high-skilled workers to favor reductions in immigration. This pattern is consistent with the adverse labor-market consequences for less-skilled workers of admitting more foreign workers. Evidence presented in chapter 3 suggests that taxpayers who bear the fiscal costs of immigration may have an incentive to join low-skilled workers in favoring the closing of US borders. This chapter will outline what economic theory has to say about who will support and who will oppose immigration. I will then use data from the 1992 and 2000 American National Election Studies (NES) surveys to examine how individuals' views on immigration vary with their exposure to labor-market competition and public-finance pressures due to immigration. This analysis, which draws on the framework and results of Hanson, Scheve, and Slaughter (2005), will help characterize the political coalitions that are likely to form for and against open immigration policies.

Individual Preferences on Immigration Policy

To predict individual opinions about admitting foreigners to the United States, I will examine how immigration affects the determinants of an individual's income. This analysis, though simple, links the labor-market and public-finance impacts of immigration to individual well-being.

Individuals receive income from wages and salaries, the profits of businesses they own, interest or capital gains on investments, and transfers from the government in cash and in goods and services. The first three items are the main sources of individuals' pre-tax income. What individuals take home—their after-tax income—consists of pre-tax income less contributions to state and federal income taxes and payroll taxes. In sum, an individuals' total income has three components:

$$\text{Total income} = \text{pre-tax income} + \text{government transfers} - \text{tax payments}.$$

To relate an individual's total income to his or her overall well-being, it is important to acknowledge that the available data sources never report all the factors that affect individual outcomes. A simple way to signify such other factors is to express well-being as the sum of an individual's total income and other residual factors, denoted as E:

$$\text{Well-being} = \text{total income} + E.$$

The new term, E, encompasses multiple factors that vary individually, including the degree to which prevailing public policies reflect the individual's beliefs and preferences. For some people, E might include nonmonetary considerations, such as the impact of immigration on culture. Political conservatives may oppose immigration on ideological grounds even if they themselves benefit monetarily from open borders. Similarly, political liberals, multiculturalists, and members of families recently arrived in the United States may favor immigration even if it is not in their own economic self-interest. When it comes to empirical analysis, it will be important to account for these noneconomic considerations as fully as possible.

To return to the determinants of income, the difference between government transfers and tax payments represents the net fiscal transfer from the government to an individual, which may be positive or negative. Rewriting total income in terms of the net fiscal transfer changes the expression for well-being to

Well-being = pre-tax income + net fiscal transfer + E,

which reflects earnings in factor markets (pre-tax income), net receipts from the government (net fiscal transfers), and residual factors (E).

Naturally, pre-tax income is likely to be higher for individuals who are more skilled or possess greater financial assets or real-estate holdings. Net fiscal transfers are likely to be positive for low-income individuals, who tend to pay relatively little in taxes and to be eligible for cash benefits, Medicaid, the Earned Income Tax Credit, and other forms of assistance. Net fiscal transfers are likely to be negative for high-income individuals, who tend to make large tax payments and to be ineligible for means-tested benefits. Both low-income and high-income individuals and their families enjoy many types of public services that are not means-tested and not contingent on earnings, such as national defense, public safety, roads and bridges, public schools, parks and public spaces, and the like.

How does immigration affect individual well-being? To make our analysis concrete, let us compare the effects of immigration on two native-born individuals, a business executive with a college degree and a janitor who never finished high school. Both are men, live in Houston, and have two children and a wife who is not employed outside the home. Both are contemplating the impact of a 10-percent decrease in immigration on the family's well-being. The total impact of immigration on well-being equals the sum of its impacts on the three components:

Change in well-being due
to a 10-percent decrease in immigration =
change in pre-tax income +
change in net fiscal transfer + change in E.

Consider the janitor. Immigration is concentrated among the low-skilled, and Texas is a high-immigration state. Thus a reduction in immigration would mean a smaller supply of low-skilled labor in Texas and less competition for the janitor in the labor market. This outcome would tend to raise his hourly wage and thus his pre-tax income. What about his net fiscal transfer? The janitor's low income may qualify him or his family for one or more types of social assistance. Since Texas neither provides generous benefits nor gives immigrants access to many benefits, as we saw in figure 3.2, a reduction in immigration would be unlikely to change the state supply of social assistance by much. Thus reduced immigration would not greatly affect any public benefits the janitor's family receives, leaving his net fiscal transfer more or less unchanged. As for a change in E, it is impossible to determine without knowledge of the janitor's beliefs and values. As a residual term, the average change in E (after netting out the component that is common across individuals) is by definition zero, though it may be large in either direction for particular individuals. In sum, reduced immigration is likely to raise the janitor's pre-tax earnings and leave his net fiscal transfer unchanged, resulting in an improvement in his family's economic well-being. On purely economic grounds, the janitor appears likely to support greater restrictions on immigration.

A decrease in immigration is likely to benefit the executive less. Though a substantial fraction of immigrants are college-educated, these individuals apparently tend to specialize in engineering, medicine, math and science, and other technical areas. Thus reduced immigration would be unlikely to affect the competition that the executive faces in the market for managerial labor. By raising wages for low-skilled labor, however, reduced immigration would increase the labor costs the executive incurs in running his business and maintaining his home. Therefore reduced immigration is likely to reduce his pre-tax income. Again, because Texas does not provide generous benefits to immigrants and lacks a progressive income tax, a reduction in immigration would not lower his tax bill much, leaving the net fiscal transfer he makes to other households more or less unchanged. In sum, reduced immigration would be likely to undermine the executive's economic well-being. All else being equal, the janitor would be more likely than the executive to favor increased restrictions on immigration.

How would the outcome change if the janitor and the executive lived in California instead of Texas? California is also a high-immigration state, but unlike Texas it offers generous public benefits, makes many of these benefits available to immigrants, and finances them in part through a progressive state income tax. Reduced immigration would decrease the net fiscal drain on the state, leading to some combination of increased public services (perhaps including social assistance) and decreased taxes. For the janitor, reduced immigration would raise pre-tax income, as in Texas, but might also raise the net fiscal transfer he receives (if California uses part of the resulting fiscal gain to fund an increase in social assistance). If his net fiscal transfer rises, he would enjoy a larger increase in economic well-being in California than he would in Texas. Thus low-skilled, low-income workers in states that are generous toward immigrants may be more supportive of immigration restrictions than similarly situated workers in states that are not generous toward immigrants.

As for the executive, reduced immigration is likely to lower his pre-tax income, as in Texas, but might also lower his net fiscal transfer to other households (if California uses part of the resulting fiscal gain to support a decrease in tax rates). This outcome would yield a smaller decrease (or larger increase) in the executive's well-being than in Texas. Among high-skilled, high-income workers, support for restrictive immigration policies is likely to be higher in states that are more generous toward immigrants.

To sum up the argument, there are two broad economic motivations for opposition to immigration. One is concern that immigration increases labor supply and thus exerts downward pressure on wages. Because low skills predominate among immigrants, low-skilled native workers are likely to be the population group most opposed to immigration on the basis of its labor-market consequences. Such opposition is likely to be most intense in high-immigration regions. A second motivation for opposition to immigration is its effect on public finances. States with large immigrant populations and generous welfare policies toward immigrants are likely to bear the highest fiscal costs associated with immigration. Individuals in more generous states are likely to be more opposed to a given level of immigration than individuals in less generous states. The more generous the state (and the more progressive the state's taxation of income), the stronger the opposition of individuals in high-income brackets is likely to be.

Public Opinion on Immigration

The NES surveys (Sapiro et al. 1998) contain extensive surveys of current political opinions based on an individual-level stratified random sample of the US population. These surveys report details about respondents' political values and beliefs, as well as their age, gender, race, ethnicity, educational attainment, occupation, industry of employment, and other characteristics. Regarding immigration, the NES asks,

> Do you think the number of immigrants from foreign countries who are permitted to come to the United States to live should be increased a little, increased a lot, decreased a little, decreased a lot, or left the same as it is now?

Data from the 1992 and 2000 NES jointly provide 3,400 observations on native-born US adults. I classify a respondent as favoring restrictions on immigration if he or she answers that the number of immigrants admitted to the country should be decreased either a little or a lot. This question calls for a respondent to reveal his or her general position on the proper direction for US immigration policy; it does not ask about the skill mix of immigrants affected by the policy. I make the assumption that respondents think any change in immigrant inflows would change the relative supply of less-skilled workers in the labor force, consistent with recent immigration patterns discussed in chapter 2.[1]

---

1. There are many reasons to be uneasy about the quality of the data in surveys of individual attitudes toward public policy. See Scheve and Slaughter (2001a) for an excellent discussion of how to interpret opinion surveys on changes in immigration policy or trade policy.

First, I examine the fraction of native-born respondents who favored new restrictions on immigration in 1992 and 2000 by three levels of education: those without a high-school diploma, those with a high-school diploma but not a college degree (who may have attended college), and those with a college degree. By virtue of their own skill profile, high-school dropouts are the group most exposed to the labor-market consequences of immigration; by virtue of their income-earning potential, college graduates are the group most exposed to the public-finance consequences of immigration. An alternative approach would be to classify individuals by income rather than education. Labor economists consider education a better indicator than income of the types of individuals with whom a respondent competes in the labor market. Income may fluctuate over time or across regions in response to economic shocks that also affect individual opinions about public policy, thereby complicating the analysis. Since education is highly correlated with income, the results are very similar if I use income level instead.

Preferences by Level of Education

Overall, the fraction of respondents favoring reductions in immigration was 50 percent in 1992 and 48 percent in 2000 (see table 4.1). In both years, the most highly educated were the least opposed to immigration. In 2000, the fraction of college graduates favoring reductions in immigration was 34 percent. That year, high-school dropouts were the most strongly opposed to immigration, with 59 percent favoring greater restrictions on the number of foreigners admitted. In 2000, the implied differential in support for immigration restrictions between high-school dropouts and college graduates was 26 percent, up from 8 percent in 1992.[2]

Why does educational attainment help predict opposition to immigration? Scheve and Slaughter (2001c) argue that low-skilled natives' opposition to immigration is attributable to the fact that their wages have been the most adversely affected by recent immigrant inflows. This interpretation is consistent with the theory presented earlier in this chapter. An alternative possibility is that education is correlated with political beliefs. More-educated individuals may be more tolerant of foreigners or more open to interacting with individuals from other ethnic groups (Hainmueller and Hiscox 2004), and thus less opposed to immigration. Based on the information in table 4.1, both interpretations appear valid. Gauging which has more empirical traction calls for a deeper analysis of the data.

---

2. These changes and those reported below are all statistically significant at conventional levels. (The one exception is the differential between high-immigration and low-immigration states in college graduates' support for immigration restrictions in 2000, reported in table 4.2.)

Table 4.1   Support for immigration restrictions by level of education, all respondents, 1992 and 2000 (percent)

Year	No high-school diploma	High-school diploma	College degree	Total
1992	47.7	55.0	39.3	50.2
2000	59.4	52.7	33.6	47.5

Notes: The data represent percentages of native-born respondents who stated a preference for reducing immigration by a little or a lot. *No high-school diploma* refers to respondents with up to 12 years of education but no diploma; *high school diploma* refers to those with 12 to 15 years of education; *college degrees* identifies those with 16 or more years of education.

Source: Sapiro et al. (1998).

Preferences by Size of a State's Immigrant Population

To determine whether the relation between education and opposition to immigration is grounded in economic concerns, I distinguished respondents living in states with large immigrant populations (over 10 percent of the state population, the mean national share in 2000) from those in states with small immigrant populations (less than 10 percent of the population).[3] Table 4.2 adds this regional dimension to the data in table 4.1.

Consider high-school dropouts. In 1992, 53 percent of high-school dropouts in high-immigration states favored restrictions on immigration, compared to 45 percent in low-immigration states. This amounts to an 8 percent differential between high- and low-immigration states (compare rows a and b in column 1). In 2000, the differential rose to 16 percent: 68 percent in high-immigration states and 52 percent in low-immigration states (compare rows c and d in column 1). The low-skilled thus appear to be much more uniformly opposed to immigration in states where they are likely to face greater labor-market competition from immigrants. They also appear to have become increasingly opposed to immigration over time: support for immigration restrictions rose by 15 percent (68 – 53) in high-immigration states and 7 percent (52 – 45) in low-immigration states. The time dimension is important, since labor-market competition from low-skilled immigrants increased considerably during the 1990s. Both across regions and over time, the opposition to immigration of low-skilled natives appears to

---

3. These results are not very sensitive to how high-immigration states are defined. In unreported results, I tried alternative splits of the data, classifying states as high-immigration based on threshold immigrant population shares of 12.5, 15, or 17.5 percent; on year-specific thresholds (equal to the national mean immigrant population share for that year); and on thresholds specific to the year and education category of the respondent (the national mean immigrant population share in the respondent's education group for that year). The results for each of these splits are strikingly similar to those reported in tables 4.1 through 4.4.

Table 4.2   Support for immigration restrictions by level of education and size of state immigrant population, 1992 and 2000 (percent)

Year	Size of state immigrant population	(1) No high-school diploma	(2) High-school diploma	(3) College degree
1992	(a) Low	45.4	55.3	38.3
	(b) High	52.9	54.5	40.3
2000	(c) Low	52.1	55.5	33.2
	(d) High	68.4	49.8	33.9

Notes: The data represent percentages of native-born respondents who stated a preference for reducing immigration by a little or a lot. *No high-school diploma* refers to respondents with up to 12 years of education but no diploma; *high-school diploma* refers to those with 12 to 15 years of education; *college degree* identifies those with 16 or more years of education.

In states with high immigrant populations, immigrants represent over 0.104 percent of the population (the US mean in 2000). States with high immigrant access to public assistance are those listed in the four upper-right cells of figure 3.2.

Source: Sapiro et al. (1998).

be strongest where labor-market competition from immigrants is most intense.

Among college graduates, opposition to immigration is also stronger in high-immigration states, but the regional differential is much weaker than for high-school dropouts. In 1992, 40 percent of college graduates in high-immigration states favored restrictions on immigration, compared to 38 percent in low-immigration states, a differential of 2 percent. In 2000, the regional differential was again small: Support for immigration restrictions dropped to 34 percent in high-immigration states and 33 percent in low-immigration states. Over time, it appears, more-skilled workers became less opposed to immigration. One possible explanation is that welfare reform softened high-skilled, high-income individuals' opposition to immigration. I will evaluate additional evidence on this interpretation below.

Preferences by Immigrants' Access to Public Services

The size of a state's immigrant population is only part of the story about the economic consequences of immigration. Though labor-market effects are likely to be more pronounced in states with larger immigrant populations, the public-finance consequences depend not just on the size of the immigrant population but also on immigrants' eligibility for public services. As we saw in figure 3.2, high-skilled, high-income workers are more exposed to the fiscal consequences of immigration in states like California than in states like Texas. It makes sense, then, to further differentiate states by the generosity of their welfare programs. Table 4.3 distinguishes respondents

Table 4.3 Support for immigration restrictions by level of education, size of state immigrant population, and immigrant access to public assistance, 1992 and 2000 (percent)

| | | Size of state immigrant population | | | | | |
| | | No high-school diploma | | High-school diploma | | College degree | |
Year	Immigrant access to public assistance	(1) Low	(2) High	(3) Low	(4) High	(5) Low	(6) High
1992	(a) Low	42.3	51.1	54.2	56.1	39.9	30.8
	(b) High	53.7	61.8	58.5	52.3	32.9	48.1
2000	(c) Low	53.1	68.0	56.3	50.2	34.0	30.3
	(d) High	46.2	69.2	52.6	49.3	30.6	37.4

Notes: The data represent percentages of native-born respondents who stated a preference for reducing immigration by a little or a lot. *No high-school diploma* refers to respondents with up to 12 years of education but no diploma; *high-school diploma* refers to those with 12 to 15 years of education; *college degree* identifies those with 16 or more years of education.

In states with high immigrant populations, immigrants represent over 0.104 percent of the population (the US mean in 2000). States with high immigrant access to public assistance are those listed in the four upper-right cells of figure 3.2.

Source: Sapiro et al. (1998).

along four dimensions: year, education, size of the state's immigration population, and that population's access to social assistance. I classify access to social assistance as high if the state falls into one the four upper-right cells in figure 3.2—that is, if the state provides more generous public benefits and makes those benefits more available to immigrant households.

Among high-school dropouts, opinions on immigration policy depend strongly on the size of the state immigrant population, as we saw in table 4.2. High-school dropouts' support for restrictions on immigration is much stronger in states with large immigrant populations, regardless of immigrants' level of access to public benefits. The differential between high-immigration and low-immigration states in the level of high-school dropouts' support for immigration restrictions (compare columns 1 and 2 by row in table 4.3) is similar in high-access and low-access states, ranging only from 8 percent to 9 percent in 1992 and from 15 percent to 23 percent in 2000. In contrast, the differential between high-access and low-access states (compare rows a and b and rows c and d in column 1) reveals no discernible pattern over time. For high-school dropouts, the potential labor-market consequences of immigration appear to be a strong predictor of support for immigration restrictions. However, there is no consistent evidence that their opinions on immigration are related to immigrants' access to public assistance.

Among college graduates, what appears to matter for preferences on immigration policy is the interaction between the size of the immigrant population and immigrants' access to public benefits. In neither 1992 nor 2000 is there a consistent difference in support for immigration restrictions between low-immigration and high-immigration states (compare columns 5 and 6 in rows a and b or in rows c and d) or between low-access and high-access states (compare rows a and b or rows c and d in columns 5 and 6). In both years, however, support for immigration restrictions is strongest in states that are both high-immigration and high-access. In high-immigration states, college graduates' support for immigration restrictions is higher in high-access states by 17 percent in 1992 (compare rows a and b in column 6) and by 7 percent in 2000 (compare rows c and d in column 6). Similarly, in high-access states, support for immigration restrictions was higher in high-immigration states by 15 percent in 1992 (compare columns 5 and 6 in row b) and by 7 percent in 2000 (compare columns 5 and 6 in row d).

In high-immigration/high-access states, more-educated workers are relatively exposed to the fiscal costs associated with immigration by virtue of their high incomes. If college graduates were uniformly more supportive of immigration restrictions across all high-immigration states—irrespective of their generosity—there would be no indication that the fiscal burden of immigration motivates their opposition to admitting foreigners. Similarly, were college graduates uniformly more supportive of immigration restrictions across all high-access states—irrespective of the size of the state immigrant population—it would also be difficult to make inferences from this test about the motivations for their policy preferences. That high-skilled individuals' opposition to immigration is strongest in states where immigrants represent a larger fiscal burden, and not simply in states where immigrants have a larger presence, suggests that the public-finance consequences of immigration are an important factor in shaping their policy preferences.

Table 4.3 also provides clues about why high-skilled workers' support for immigration restrictions has fallen over time. Among college graduates, the largest reduction in support for immigration restrictions occurred in high-immigration/high-access states (compare rows b and d in column 6). This decline of 11 percent accounts for much of the overall decline in college-graduate support for immigration restrictions evident in table 4.1. Natives in high-immigration/high-access states were those most likely to benefit from federal welfare reform's restrictions on immigrant access to public benefits. As was seen in figure 3.1, usage of social assistance by immigrant households declined relative to that of native households for all categories except Medicaid after welfare reform.

One interpretation of the results in table 4.3 is that welfare reform reduced high-income respondents' exposure to the fiscal costs of immigration, softening their support for immigration restrictions. Obviously, one

Table 4.4 Support for immigration restrictions excluding very conservative and very liberal respondents, 1992 and 2000 (percent)

| | | Size of state immigrant population | | | | | |
| | | No high-school diploma | | High-school diploma | | College degree | |
Year	Immigrant access to public assistance	(1) Low	(2) High	(3) Low	(4) High	(5) Low	(6) High
1992	(a) Low	43.3	52.4	54.3	55.8	39.1	30.2
	(b) High	51.3	56.7	58.9	53.2	33.8	46.7
2000	(c) Low	53.9	67.4	58.6	52.5	32.8	30.1
	(d) High	46.2	70.8	52.4	50.6	30.8	36.6

Notes: The data represent percentages of native-born respondents who stated a preference for reducing immigration by a little or a lot. *No high-school diploma* refers to respondents with up to 12 years of education but no diploma; *high-school diploma* refers to those with 12 to 15 years of education; *college degree* identifies those with 16 or more years of education.

In states with high immigrant populations, immigrants represent over 0.104 percent of the population (the US mean in 2000). States with high immigrant access to public assistance are those listed in the four upper-right cells of figure 3.2.

Source: Sapiro et al. (1998).

should be cautious about such an interpretation. During the 1990s many other factors changed across states, and table 4.3 controls only for education, the size of a state's immigrant population, and immigrants' access to state benefits. As I will discuss below, the large decline in support for immigration restrictions among college graduates in high-immigration/high-access states holds up in regression analysis when additional controls are introduced (Hanson, Scheve, and Slaughter 2005). Nevertheless, there may be other influential factors for which I have not accounted. This leaves us with intriguing but still tentative evidence that welfare reform may have reduced support for immigration restrictions.

The Relationship Between Preferences and Ideology

Tables 4.1 through 4.3 do not control for the political beliefs and values of respondents. More conservative individuals may choose not to live in states with large immigrant populations or generous public benefits; more liberal individuals may be more willing to live in high-immigration states or those with generous benefits. A related possibility is that the political beliefs of a state's native residents affect how friendly its policies are toward immigrants. Both possibilities could artificially inflate observed regional differences in public opinion about immigration policy.

To control for the possible effects of ideology on my results, table 4.4 replicates table 4.3 but excludes individuals who describe themselves as either very conservative or very liberal; these two groups jointly account for 10 percent of the sample. The pattern of support for restrictions on immigration shown in table 4.4 is very similar to that in table 4.3. Thus ideology does not appear to be driving the results reported in tables 4.1 through 4.3. Even excluding individuals who describe themselves as conservative to very conservative and liberal to very liberal—38 percent of respondents—the results are very similar.

Econometric Analysis of Individual Preferences

Even with controls for ideology, the analysis reported so far is somewhat crude. A more rigorous approach would be to model individual preferences on immigration policy econometrically. Hanson, Scheve, and Slaughter (2005) use the 1992 and 2000 NES data to estimate the probability that a given respondent favors restrictions on immigration as a function of individual characteristics (age, education, gender, race, ethnicity, ideology, employment status), characteristics of the state in which the respondent lives (size of the immigrant population, generosity toward immigrants), and other factors. Their results are consistent with those presented here, suggesting that additional controls would not change the key qualitative findings.

Hanson, Scheve, and Slaughter find stronger support for restrictions on immigration among the less educated, whites, union workers, unemployed workers, and political conservatives. Clearly, individual circumstances matter in policy preferences. Support for immigration restrictions is also stronger in states with larger immigrant populations and those where immigrants have greater access to public benefits. In high-immigration states, it is the least-skilled individuals who are relatively more opposed to immigration. This finding is consistent with the hypothesis that political opposition to immigration arises in part from its impact on labor-market competition. In those states characterized by both larger immigrant populations and greater generosity, it is the more skilled who are relatively more opposed to immigration. In these states, opposition to immigration may be due in part to its effects on the net fiscal burdens of existing native residents. Between 1992 and 2000, less-skilled natives became more opposed and high-skilled natives became less opposed to immigration. Again, there are important differences in these changes across states. In high-immigration/high-access states, most skill groups became less opposed to immigration; the largest changes occurred among college graduates, the group most exposed to the fiscal effects of immigration on income taxes. This finding is consistent with the hypothesis that welfare reform has softened opposition to immigration in states where the fiscal consequences of immigration are most acute. In sum, though political beliefs almost surely play a role in opinions on immigration policy, the education cleavage seems very consistent with economic concern about labor-market and public-finance pressures.[4]

The economic consequences of immigration appear to affect public opinion about admitting foreigners to the United States. Individuals are more supportive of restrictions on immigration if they are more exposed to the labor-market consequences of immigration—as are low-skilled natives in states with large immigrant populations—or to the public-finance consequences of immigration—as are high-skilled natives in states with large immigrant populations and generous public assistance for immigrants. There is some evidence, however, that changes in policy affect individual policy preferences. After welfare reform, which restricted immigrants' access to public benefits, opposition to immigration fell among those most exposed to the fiscal costs of admitting foreigners. It appears that one key to generating greater support for immigration would be to reduce its adverse effects on the labor-market earnings and fiscal burdens of US residents.

---

4. See Scheve and Slaughter (2001a, 2001c) and Hanson, Scheve, and Slaughter (2005) for further discussion.

5

Reforming US Immigration Policy

Political gridlock currently prevails regarding US immigration policy. This state of affairs makes it difficult to address pressing issues related to illegal immigration and national security: what to do about the 10 million illegal immigrants living in the country, and how to get immigration authorities and intelligence agencies to coordinate meaningfully with one another. There is currently no majority coalition supporting efforts to resolve these problems. Even with his party in control of the executive and legislative branches of government, President Bush's attempts to reform immigration policy have so far been unsuccessful.

The results reported in chapter 4 highlight two sources of opposition to immigration: concern about labor-market pressures and concern about public finances. Naturally, those who believe that immigration depresses their wages or increases their net tax burden are likely to oppose admitting more foreigners. To a large extent, the labor-market consequences of immigration are inescapable. By definition, immigration increases the supply of labor, which will tend to reduce the wages of native workers subject to replacement by incoming foreign workers. The only way to eliminate the labor-market consequences of immigration is to reduce the number of foreigners admitted to the country.[1] By contrast, the adverse

---

1. Conceivably, workers hurt by immigration could be compensated by taxing those who gain. In practice, such specific redistributive schemes appear to be hard to implement. The Earned Income Tax Credit (EITC), however, is an existing policy that protects low-income workers against negative wage shocks (from any source). When the EITC credit exceeds taxes owed, eligible taxpayers (who must have a valid Social Security number) receive a refund. In 2004, the income cutoffs for eligibility were $11,490 for an unmarried taxpayer with no children and $30,388 for an unmarried taxpayer with one child. For poor native workers,

public-finance consequences of immigration are controllable by public policy. If the impact of immigration on the net tax burden of US natives were reduced, it might be possible to forge a coalition behind meaningful policy reform.

There are at least two strategies for policy reform that would dampen immigration's consequences for public finances. One is to change the skill composition of those admitted. By shifting to a system that favors high-skilled immigrants, the United States would attract individuals likely to pay more in taxes than they draw in public services. A second strategy is to restructure immigrants' rights to public benefits. If immigrants were prohibited from drawing on public assistance and certain other public services for a designated period after entering the country, the fiscal drain associated with immigration would be smaller. Either policy would implicitly favor immigrants intending to work over those intending to obtain public benefits.

Tentative moves toward favoring high-skilled immigrants and restricting immigrants' access to public benefits have been made in the last decade. H-1B visas allow high-skilled immigrants to work in the United States for up to six years, mainly in the software and electronics industries. In 2000, at the height of the technology boom, Congress temporarily increased the annual number of H-1B visas from 115,000 to 195,000.[2] Welfare reform in 1996 in effect imposed a five-year waiting period—the interval between obtaining permanent residence and becoming eligible to apply for citizenship—before immigrants gain access to many government benefits.

This chapter will examine options for reforming US immigration policy. Following a discussion of recent proposals, I will evaluate the relative merits of a skills-based and a rights-based immigration policy.

Proposals for Immigration Reform

In an economy without distortions associated with market failure or public-policy interventions, the optimal immigration policy would be open borders.[3] The logic of free immigration is analogous to the logic of free trade. Both contribute to the equalization of prices for factors and goods across borders, which promotes economic efficiency and helps create the conditions for global welfare to be maximized. Barriers to the movement of

---

the group apparently most affected by labor-market competition from low-skilled immigrants, the EITC offers some protection against policy changes that reduce earnings. For a theoretical analysis of options to protect low-wage workers from immigration, see Sinn (2004). Wage subsidies, of which the EITC is one type, are the least inefficient policy option among those considered.

2. In 2003, after several years of slow economic growth, Congress allowed the number of H-1B visas to fall to 65,000. For more detail, see http://uscis.gov/graphics/publicaffairs/.

3. This argument ignores any perceived negative cultural consequences of immigration.

goods or factors lead to inefficient outcomes and leave gains from trade unexploited. Such barriers tend to cause labor-abundant countries like Mexico to have low wages for labor and high relative prices for capital-intensive goods, and capital-abundant countries like the United States to have high wages for labor and high relative prices for labor-intensive goods. In theory, it is possible to achieve efficiency either through free trade or through free immigration, which led Robert Mundell (1957) to conclude that international trade in goods and international movements of factors substitute for one another.

We are, of course, far from a world without distortions. Population growth—whether due to immigration or to other sources—tends to exacerbate distortions associated with poorly defined property rights over air, waterways, highways, and common areas. More people inevitably mean more pollution and more congestion. An increase in the number of low-income people tends to exacerbate distortions associated with welfare policies, prompting Milton Friedman to declare, "It's just obvious that you can't have free immigration and a welfare state."[4] The presence of these and other distortions means that the United States is setting immigration policy in a less-than-ideal world. In such an environment, it seems likely that a policy of less-than-free immigration would be the constrained optimum (Wellisch and Walz 1998).

Distortions also exacerbate political conflict over immigration. Some US environmentalists oppose immigration because it contributes to population growth. Some fiscal conservatives oppose immigration in the belief that it increases the pool of people who use US welfare programs. Even ignoring distortions, the redistributive effects of immigration create political conflict. Immigration redistributes income between factors of production, raising incomes for some (such as owners of capital) and lowering it for others (such as low-skilled labor). Labor unions' long-standing opposition to immigration, reversed only in the 1990s when unions began to recruit more actively among recent immigrants, derives in part from immigration's perceived negative effects on blue-collar workers.

Proposals to reform immigration policy tend to focus on minimizing either immigration's effect on distortions or its redistributive effects on income. Since the redistributive effects of immigration are unavoidable, policies that attempt to limit immigration's exacerbative effect on existing distortions are likely to be more appealing on efficiency grounds.

A variety of proposals have emerged in recent years, both inside and outside government, for reform of US immigration policy. President Bush's plan, known as Fair and Secure Immigration Reform (FSIR), would offer amnesty to some illegal immigrants and expand the number of temporary work visas granted to laborers from Mexico. Little has yet been said about

---

4. Peter Brimelow, "Milton Friedman, Soothsayer," *Hoover Digest* 2 (1998). www.hoover. stanford.edu/publications/digest/982/friedman3.html.

how the president's plan would change permanent legal immigration or enforcement against illegal immigration. Congress is also considering legislation on immigration. In 2003 Senators Edward Kennedy (D-MA) and Larry Craig (R-ID) proposed the Agricultural Job, Opportunity, Benefits, and Security Act (AgJobs). AgJobs would offer amnesty to illegal immigrants who had worked on US farms in the preceding 12 months. It would also reform the H-2A visa program for temporary agricultural workers by expanding the number of visas awarded and creating a mechanism for employers to bring in foreign agricultural workers more easily (www.senate .gov/~gsmith/agjob.htm#a). In 2004, Democratic members of the House of Representatives proposed the Safe, Orderly Legal Visas and Enforcement Act (SOLVE), which would legalize unauthorized workers who have been in the United States for at least five years, create a transitional work visa for those who have been in the country for less than five years, and expand the number of low-skilled temporary work visas to 350,000. The executive, Senate, and House plans all focus to varying degrees on temporary visas and amnesty for illegal immigrants. None offers specifics on how to modify enforcement to reduce illegal immigration.

A decade ago, the Commission on Immigration Reform—created by the Immigration Act of 1990 and known as the Jordan Commission after its chair, Barbara Jordan—produced an influential set of recommendations to limit family-based immigration to immediate family members, abolish unskilled legal immigration, expand border and interior enforcement against illegal immigration (including a verifiable identification system), make all legal immigrants (including noncitizens) eligible for public benefits, and promote the Americanization of immigrants (Jordan 1995).

So far, none of these proposals has come close to becoming law. Of the four, only that of the Jordan Commission offers a systematic approach to the level and composition of immigration, the rights granted to immigrants, and enforcement against illegal immigration. It would move the United States decisively in the direction of a skills-based immigration policy, which is also advocated by Borjas (1999a), Huntington (2004), and others.

A Skills-Based Immigration Policy

A skills-based immigration policy would radically alter the mix of individuals admitted to the United States. It would severely limit immigration based on family reunification. The effects on the US economy would probably also be profound. Incoming legal immigrants would be much less likely to use means-tested entitlement programs. Since higher-income individuals also tend to have smaller families, such a policy shift would also reduce immigration's total contribution to population growth (even if the annual number of immigrants admitted to the country remained the same). Low-skilled native workers would probably see their wages increase both in absolute terms and relative to high-skilled workers, reducing earnings inequality in the United States.

One disadvantage of such a policy is that high-skilled immigration would tend to work against globalization. Because the United States is already abundant in skills and capital relative to the rest of the world, admitting primarily high-skilled workers would sharpen international differences in relative factor supplies. This shift would tend to increase the wage difference for less-skilled workers between the United States and the rest of the world and to move the world further from factor-price equalization. Such a move could lower global economic efficiency and welfare.[5] Poor countries' loss of high-skilled labor could have negative effects on their GDPs and on the performance of their political, legal, and educational institutions.

Another disadvantage for poor countries is that high-skilled emigrants appear less likely than low-skilled emigrants to remit income to their families at home (Orozco 2003). Remittances help offset poor countries' loss in GDP due to the labor outflow associated with emigration. For Mexico, Prachi Mishra (2003) estimates that between 1970 and 2000 emigration increased average wages by 8 percent. By 2000, the number of Mexican emigrants in the United States was equal to 16 percent of the labor force in Mexico. Based on these figures, Mexico's emigration loss in 2000 was 0.5 percent of its GDP. In Mexico's case, however, this loss is more than offset by the income that emigrants remit to family in Mexico, which in 2003 was 2 percent of GDP. On net, residents of Mexico—those who do not emigrate—appear to gain from emigration, with much of the gain presumably flowing to the families of emigrants via remittances. In some countries remittances represent an even larger share of economic activity, exceeding 10 percent of 2003 GDP in Belize, the Dominican Republic, El Salvador, Guyana, Haiti, Honduras, Jamaica, and Nicaragua (IADB 2004). The Inter-American Development Bank finds that in 2003 Latin American immigrants in the United States sent a total of $31 billion to their home countries, amounting to 1.4 percent of the region's GDP. If poor countries were to send high-skilled rather than low-skilled labor abroad, remittances could decrease, thus reducing their GDPs.

Furthermore, shifting from low-skilled to high-skilled immigration might not have the profound effects on US labor markets that some proponents expect. If the United States took in fewer low-skilled workers from poor countries, wage differentials between the United States and

---

5. In a Heckscher-Ohlin trade model, high-skilled immigration to high-skilled countries would increase international factor-price differences and decrease global welfare. But such a model envisions no incentive for such migration, because wages for high-skilled labor would be lower in skill-abundant countries. This is not the case in the United States: US workers' wages appear to be higher than wages for workers in poor countries in all skill categories, which probably reflects superior US technology. In a world characterized by cross-country differences in technology, how migration affects global welfare depends on how such migration affects the creation and diffusion of technology.

these countries would probably increase. This shift would tend to increase both US demand for imports from poor countries and poor-country demand for US capital. By reducing the import of labor from Mexico, for instance, the United States would probably increase the import of goods from Mexico and the export of US capital to Mexico. In general equilibrium, these increased trade and capital flows would decrease relative demand for low-skilled US labor and partly offset the labor-market consequences of reduced low-skilled immigration, perhaps leaving low-skilled US native workers only modestly better off than they are now.

To sum up these effects, a shift to a skills-based immigration policy would be likely to reduce the fiscal costs of immigration and to narrow the wage gap between high-skilled and low-skilled labor in the United States. However, these outcomes would entail the potential cost of diminishing well-being in poor countries.

A Rights-Based Immigration Policy

A rights-based approach to reforming immigration policy would phase in immigrant access to government benefits more gradually over time. This goal could be accomplished by means of a graduated set of rights to public benefits, to which immigrants would gain access after having worked in the United States for a specific time period. One way to implement such a plan would be for new immigrants to be issued temporary work visas (of, say, three years' duration) that would give them rights to certain benefits (public education, self-financed medical benefits, participation in a self-financed pension plan) but not others (public assistance, food stamps, public housing, Medicaid). Satisfying the terms of the temporary work visa would result in automatic renewal, and, after a specified number of renewals, permanent residence. After five years as a permanent resident, an individual could apply for citizenship (as is currently the case). Such a plan—which could easily be incorporated into any of the existing proposals for immigration reform—would lengthen the interval between arrival in the United States and eligibility to draw on the full set of government-provided public benefits. This proposal would strengthen the link between admission to the United States and the desire to work, and would reduce the fiscal drain associated with immigration, relative to current policy (and existing legislative proposals).[6]

---

6. One issue in implementation would be whether to admit immediate family members of temporary visa holders. Currently, the United States allows immediate family members to join temporary visa holders on longer-term visas (such as the H-1B) but not those on shorter-term visas (such as the H-2A or H-2B). Family members are not allowed to work in the United States and are ineligible for most types of social assistance. Conformity with this precedent would entail admitting immediate family members but imposing strict limits on their ability to work and to draw public benefits.

This proposal would also carry welfare reform one step further. Current policy distinguishes between permanent residents and citizens, and makes the former ineligible for a wide range in benefits in some states. Since an individual must be a permanent resident for five years before applying for citizenship, there is already a five-year waiting period before immigrants gain full access to public benefits. A rights-based approach that required completion of one or more terms as a temporary immigrant would create a further distinction between earlier-tenure immigrants on temporary visas and later-tenure immigrants with green cards.

A likely criticism of a rights-based approach is that it would create multiple classes of US residents. Immigrants on temporary work visas would spend a number of years without access to the rights enjoyed by permanent residents, who would in turn enjoy fewer rights than citizens. Advocates for immigrants often criticize guest-worker programs for relegating immigrants to second-class status. What distinguishes a rights-based approach from other guest-worker programs is that it launches immigrants on a well-defined path toward citizenship. It would also afford greater legal certainty to illegal immigrants who chose to convert to temporary legal status.

Labor unions also complain about guest-worker programs, citing the lack of labor rights provided to immigrants. However, it would be feasible to grant temporary immigrants the full set of labor protections that apply to citizens: collective bargaining, a federally mandated minimum wage, unemployment insurance, legally mandated health and safety standards, and the like. In this case, the only difference between temporary immigrants and other workers would be that the former would lack access to the same public entitlement programs.

Employment-Based Admission and Expanded Temporary Immigration

Skills-based and rights-based immigration policies are not mutually exclusive. In principle the United States could enact both by converting family-based admission slots to employment-based admission slots and by converting illegal immigrants to temporary immigrants. Doing so would raise the average skill level of incoming immigrants and shrink the illegal-immigrant population. To pursue adoption of either policy, it would be essential to specify more detail regarding treatment of illegal immigrants, enforcement against illegal immigration, and the composition and level of immigration.

Illegal Immigrants

Temporary work visas would offer a solution to the question of how to deal with the 10 million illegal immigrants currently living in the United

States. A special pool of visas, much larger than the typical annual allotment (discussed below), could be created for illegal immigrants now residing in the United States. The granting of these visas would amount to a limited amnesty for these immigrants. Congress would have to decide which illegal immigrants would be eligible for a visa from the special pool. The most recent amnesty, for instance, offered in 1988 under the Immigration Reform and Control Act, applied to individuals who could demonstrate that they had resided in the United States continuously for the previous six years. Illegal immigrants ineligible for visas from the special pool would still be eligible to apply for regular temporary work visas, which the government would make available on an annual basis. This approach has obvious parallels to President Bush's plan and to the House and Senate plans, although none of those plans has yet specified how temporary legal immigrants would progress to permanent residence.

For an illegal immigrant to obtain a special-pool visa, an employer would have to apply on his or her behalf. This requirement would obligate many employers to admit to having employed illegal immigrants, which is tantamount to admitting violation of the law. To give employers an incentive to help their employees become temporary legal workers, it would probably be necessary to offer immunity from prosecution for certain past illegal employment practices.

Groups that traditionally oppose immigration would probably be vehement in their objections to an amnesty for illegal immigrants. It is almost inconceivable, however, that the United States could reduce the illegal-immigrant population without an amnesty of some sort. One alternative, mass deportations, would require a police effort on a scale never before seen in this country. However intense the opposition to an amnesty, opposition to mass deportations would probably be much more so. One feature of a limited amnesty that might make it more politically palatable than a blanket amnesty is that it would not lead directly to permanent residence but to a temporary work visa. Former illegal immigrants would not be eligible for full public benefits until they had completed the required number of terms as temporary immigrants and a five-year period as a permanent legal resident. Another objection to an amnesty is that it would raise the incentive for illegal immigration. This is a serious concern. To avoid inviting future illegal immigration, the United States would also have to enforce against illegal entry more effectively.

Enforcement

The enforcement policy that has been in place since the early 1990s involves heavy patrols in major cities along the Mexican border, light patrols in unpopulated zones along the same border, and minimal presence in the US interior (Boeri, Hanson, and McCormick 2002). It is noteworthy that immigration authorities do not track most temporary legal immigrants, making it difficult to determine how many individuals overstay their entry visas. The result of this policy is that, once in the United States, illegal immigrants appear to face little risk of apprehension or deportation.

Clearly, current enforcement policy is ineffective. One measure of its ineffectiveness is that, after the United States dramatically increased border enforcement in the early 1990s, illegal immigration actually increased. Average annual net illegal immigration in the 1990s was 300,000 to 500,000 individuals a year, up from 200,000 to 300,000 in the previous decade (Boeri, Hanson, and McCormick 2002). About two-thirds of illegal immigrants enter the United States by crossing the border with Mexico and about one-third overstay temporary visas.

Effective enforcement requires a strong presence at the borders, but it also requires serious enforcement efforts in the interior. Currently, immigration authorities devote few resources to investigating or monitoring employers who appear likely to hire illegal immigrants (GAO 2002). Occasional attempts to increase interior enforcement meet with fierce political opposition. Following raids of Georgia onion fields during the 1998 harvest, the INS was publicly criticized by the US Attorney General, both Georgia senators, and three members of Georgia's congressional delegation for injuring Georgia farmers (Mark Krikorian, "Lured by Jobs, Illegal Immigrants Risk Death at Border Crossings," *Santa Barbara News–Press*, April 25, 1999). The raids ceased shortly thereafter. Large-scale raids of farms in California, Florida, and Texas, the states that attract the largest concentrations of undocumented workers, are virtually unheard of. In 2000 and 2001, the INS investigated the meatpacking industry in Nebraska and Iowa, reputed to use illegal labor intensively, but made no large-scale raids on plants. Most plant visits by INS agents were announced in advance, as has become standard practice.[7]

What makes interior enforcement difficult is that employers can plausibly deny knowing that they employ illegal immigrants. They are required to ask employees for legal documents (a Social Security card, a green card) and to record this information on forms that immigration authorities can review if they audit the plant. As long as the documents appear genuine, employers are more or less free from legal liability. Since employers do not have to verify the authenticity of employee identification, this check serves only to weed out obvious forgeries.

An alternative approach would be to mandate immediate verification of an employee's legal status. Through the voluntary Basic Pilot Program,

---

7. The INS strategy was to announce plant visits, ask employers' permission to review employee records, and then interview workers whose records looked suspicious. The many workers who failed to report for their INS interviews lost their jobs. The result of the INS investigation, then, was not monetary sanctions on employers but (indirectly) forced resignations by workers. See "Immigration: In the Vanguard," *The Economist*, October 16, 1999, 31–32.

employers can currently verify the authenticity of job applicants' Social Security numbers with the Social Security Administration (SSA) and the Department of Homeland Security (DHS).[8] Thus, the SSA and DHS already have a database to which employers can submit electronic requests for information, which makes the verification process trivial. Converting electronic verification from a voluntary program to a mandatory requirement for employment would eliminate plausible deniability on the part of employers. The only way they could hire illegal immigrants would be to keep these workers off their official employment rolls, an unquestionable violation of the law. An alternative (or perhaps a complement) to mandatory electronic verification would be a national identity card, an approach likely to face political opposition from many quarters.

Mandatory verification would also make audits of employers by immigration authorities more transparent. An employer who had failed to verify an employee's Social Security status (for which there would be an electronic record) would be guilty of an infraction. With these procedures in place, a modest increase in interior enforcement could potentially greatly increase its effectiveness. The DHS would also have a record of employment for each temporary legal immigrant, which would be useful for evaluating applications for renewal of temporary work visas.

Immediate verification of an employee's legal status would not increase the information burdens on either employees or employers. Currently, employers must complete and retain I-9 identification verification forms on all employees.[9] And the technology for electronic verification of employability clearly already exists.

The Composition and Level of Immigration

A rights-based approach to immigration policy could be implemented under current immigration quotas. These quotas reserve the majority of entry slots for family members of US citizens and legal residents. The change would be that new immigrants, whether family-sponsored or employer-sponsored, would receive a temporary work visa rather than a green card. New immigrants would not become permanent residents until they had completed the required number of terms on temporary work visas. The advantage of adopting a rights-based immigration policy is that it could create political support for addressing illegal immigration, including a limited amnesty for illegal immigrants, mandatory employee verification procedures, and new enforcement capabilities.

---

8. See http://uscis.gov/graphics/services/SAVE.htm for a description of the Basic Pilot Program.

9. Employers do not have to submit these forms to the government. They must only make them available in the event of an audit by government inspectors.

However, there is no reason to believe that current admission criteria represent the constrained optimum policy choice for the United States. Neither the skill mix of new immigrants nor the current level of immigration reflects prevailing economic conditions; both are mandated by legislation that changes slowly over time. The inflexibility of existing policy makes it attractive to imagine more extensive changes in the mix and number of individuals who gain admission to the United States.

Under a rights-based program in which immigrants first enter under temporary work visas, it would be straightforward to set entry criteria according to US labor-market conditions. One possibility would be for employers to post information electronically on jobs they desire to fill with temporary immigrants. These postings would reflect the excess demand for labor in the United States. The occupational distribution of postings would in principle indicate where excess demand for labor was the greatest. Foreigners could then apply for job openings, providing information about themselves electronically to prospective employers.[10] The number of foreign applicants per position would be an indication of the excess supply of foreign labor. Occupations in which the number of applicants exceeded the number of job postings (which, realistically, could be almost all occupations) would indicate the existence of queues for jobs in the United States. The length of the electronic job queues in different occupations would indicate to immigration authorities where the economic gains to immigration might be the greatest.

To determine the overall number of immigrants admitted, immigration authorities could also use information on domestic economic conditions. Congress could set a flexible cap on total admissions, such that any excess admissions in years with strong labor demand would have to be offset by fewer admissions in years with weak labor demand. The cap could apply to the total number of temporary work visas that immigration authorities grant. Each year, the number of those with temporary immigrant status would drop as individuals either completed the required number of renewals and obtained permanent residence or had their visas revoked. These outflows would create openings for new temporary immigrants, with net total admissions determined by the flexible cap.

It has been nearly two decades since the last major reform of US immigration policy. Since that time, illegal immigration has increased, the wages of low-skilled US workers have fallen, the short-run fiscal costs of immigration have grown, and immigration has become a more contentious issue in American life. Few would disagree that a new round of policy reform is needed. Meaningful reform will have to address, at the very least, an amnesty for illegal immigrants and enforcement against

---

10. To give employers and employees an incentive to provide truthful information, it would probably be necessary to charge a fee to list employment opportunities and employment applications.

future illegal immigration. Employers will only go along with reform if they feel they will not lose access to foreign workers. The prospect of an amnesty and continuing high levels of immigration would probably face strong opposition. One strategy for softening this opposition and for forging a coalition behind reform is to convince some current opponents of immigration—such as taxpayers in high-immigration states—that reform is in their interest. It is hard to imagine that this goal could be achieved without lowering the fiscal costs associated with immigration. Distributive conflicts appear to be at the heart of disagreements over immigration policy. Fortunately, policy options are available that can lessen the distributive consequences of immigration and move the United States toward an immigration policy that better serves the national interest.

References

Bean, Frank D., Rodolf Corona, Rodolf Tuiran, Karen A. Woodrow-Lafield, and Jennifer Van Hook. 2001. Circular, Invisible, and Ambiguous Migrants. *Demography* 38, no. 3 (August): 411–22.

Bean, Frank D., Jennifer Van Hook, and Karen Woodrow-Lafield. 2001. *Estimates of Numbers of Unauthorized Migrants Residing in the United States.* Pew Hispanic Center Special Report. Washington: Pew Hispanic Center.

Bleakley, Hoyt, and Aimee Chin. 2004. Language, Skills, and Earnings: Evidence from Childhood Immigrants. *Review of Economics and Statistics* 86, no. 2: 481–96.

Boeri, Tito, Gordon Hanson, and Barry McCormick. 2002. *Immigration Policy and the Welfare System.* Oxford: Oxford University Press.

Borjas, George J. 1999a. *Heaven's Door: Immigration Policy and the American Economy.* Princeton, NJ: Princeton University Press.

Borjas, George J. 1999b. The Economic Analysis of Immigration. In *Handbook of Labor Economics*, ed. Orley C. Ashenfelter and David Card. Amsterdam: North-Holland.

Borjas, George J. 2002. *The Impact of Welfare Reform on Immigrant Welfare Use.* Washington: Center for Immigration Studies.

Borjas, George J. 2003. The Labor Demand Curve Is Downward Sloping: Reexamining the Impact of Immigration on the Labor Market. *Quarterly Journal of Economics* 118, no. 4 (November): 1335–76.

Borjas, George J., Richard B. Freeman, and Lawrence F. Katz. 1997. How Much Do Immigration and Trade Affect Labor Market Outcomes? *Brookings Papers on Economic Activity* 1: 1–90. Washington: Brookings Institution.

Borjas, George J., and Lynette Hilton. 1996. Immigration and the Welfare State: Immigrant Participation in Means-Tested Entitlement Programs. *Quarterly Journal of Economics* 111, no. 2: 575–604.

Borjas, George J., and Lawrence F. Katz. 2005. The Evolution of the Mexican-Born Workforce in the United States. Cambridge, MA: Harvard University. Photocopy.

Bureau of International Labor Affairs. 1996. *Effects of the Immigration Reform and Control Act: Characteristics and Labor Market Behavior of the Legalized Population Five Years Following Legalization.* Washington: US Department of Labor.

Calavita, Kitty. 1992. *Inside the State: The Bracero Program, Immigration, and the INS.* New York: Routledge.

Camarota, Steven A. 2002. *The Open Door: How Militant Islamic Terrorists Entered and Remained in the United States, 1993–2001.* Paper 21. Washington: Center for Immigration Studies.

Card, David. 2001. Immigrant Inflows, Native Outflows, and the Local Labor Market Impacts of Higher Immigration. *Journal of Labor Economics* 19, no. 1: 22–64.

Card, David, and Ethan Lewis. 2005 (forthcoming). The Diffusion of Mexican Immigrants in the 1990s: Patterns and Impacts. In *Mexican Immigration,* ed. George J. Borjas. Chicago, IL: University of Chicago and National Bureau of Economic Research.

Cornelius, Wayne. 2001. Death at the Border: Efficacy and Unintended Consequences of US Immigration Policy. *Population and Development Review* 27, no. 4: 661–85.

Costanzo, Joe, Cynthia Davis, Caribert Irazi, Daniel Goodkind, and Roberto Ramirez. 2001. *Evaluating Components of International Migration: The Residual Foreign Born Population.* Division Working Paper 61. Washington: US Bureau of the Census.

Council of Economic Advisers. 2005. *Economic Report of the President.* Washington: US Government Printing Office.

Daniels, Roger. 2003. *Guarding the Door: American Immigrants and Immigration Policy since 1882.* New York: Hill and Wang.

Duncan, Brian, and Stephen J. Trejo. 2005. Ethnic Identification, Intermarriage, and Unmeasured Progress by Mexican Americans. University of Texas, Austin. Photocopy.

Fix, Michael, and Jeffrey Passel. 2002. *The Scope and Impact of Welfare Reform's Immigrant Provisions.* Discussion Paper 02-03. Washington: Urban Institute.

General Accounting Office. 2002. Immigration Enforcement: Challenges to Implementing the INS Interior Enforcement Strategy. Testimony before the Subcommittee on Immigration and Claims of the House Committee on the Judiciary. February.

Grogger, Jeffrey, and Stephen J. Trejo. 2002. *Moving Behind or Moving Up? The Intergenerational Progress of Mexican Americans.* San Francisco: Public Policy Institute of California.

Hainmueller, Jens, and Michael J. Hiscox. 2004. Educated Preferences: Explaining Attitudes Toward Immigration in Europe. Paper presented at Annual Meeting of the American Political Science Association.

Hanson, Gordon H., Kenneth F. Scheve, and Matthew J. Slaughter. 2005. *Local Public Finance and Individual Preferences over Globalization Strategies.* NBER Working Paper 11028. Cambridge, MA: National Bureau of Economic Research.

Hanson, Gordon H., and Antonio Spilimbergo. 1999. Illegal Immigration, Border Enforcement and Relative Wages: Evidence from Apprehensions at the US–Mexico Border. *American Economic Review* 89: 1337–57.

Hanson, Gordon H., and Antonio Spilimbergo. 2001. Political Economy, Sectoral Shocks, and Border Enforcement. *Canadian Journal of Economics* 34: 612–38.

Huntington, Samuel. 2004. *Who Are We? The Challenges to America's National Identity.* New York: Simon and Schuster.

Inter-American Development Bank. 2004. *Sending Money Home: Remittances to Latin America and the Caribbean.* IADB Report. Washington: Inter-American Development Bank (May).

Jordan, Barbara. 1995. Testimony before the US Commission and Immigration Reform. Washington: US House of Representatives Committee on Ways and Means, Subcommittee on Human Resources (March 29).

Kossoudji, Sherrie A., and Deborah A. Cobb-Clark. 2002. Coming Out of the Shadows: Learning about Legal Status and Wages from the Legalized Population. *Journal of Labor Economics* 20, no. 3 (July): 598–628.

Mayda, Anna Maria. 2004. *Who Is Against Immigration? A Cross-Country Investigation of Individual Attitudes Toward Immigrants.* IZA Discussion Paper 1115. Centro Studi Luca d'Agliano Development Working Paper 187. http://ssrn.com/abstract=533802.

Mayda, Anna Maria, and Dani Rodrik. 2002. *Why Are Some People (and Countries) More Protectionist Than Others?* NBER Working Paper 8461. Cambridge, MA: National Bureau of Economic Research.

Mishra, Prachi. 2003. Emigration and Wages in Source Countries: Evidence from Mexico. New York: Columbia University. Photocopy.

Mundell, Robert. 1957. International Trade and Factor Mobility. *American Economic Review* 47: 321–35.

O'Rourke, Kevin, and Richard Sinnott. 2001. The Determinants of Individual Trade Policy Preferences: International Survey Evidence. In *Brookings Trade Forum: 2001*, ed. S.M. Collins and D. Rodrik. Washington: Brookings Institution.

O'Rourke, Kevin, and Richard Sinnott. 2003. *Migration Flows: Political Economy of Migration and the Empirical Challenges*. Discussion Paper Series iiisdp06. Dublin: Institute for International Integration Studies.

Orozco, Manuel. 2003. *Worker Remittances in an International Scope*. Inter-American Dialogue Research Series. Washington: Inter-American Development Bank.

Passel, Jeffrey S. 2005. *Estimates of the Size and Characteristics of the Undocumented Population*. Washington: Pew Hispanic Center.

Passel, Jeffrey S., Randy Capps, and Michael Fix. 2004. *Undocumented Immigrants: Facts and Figures*. Washington: Urban Institute.

Passel, Jeffrey S., and Wendy Zimmerman. 2001. Are Immigrants Leaving California? Settlement Patterns of Immigrants in the Late 1990s. Washington: Urban Institute. Photocopy.

Rodrik, Dani. 1997. *Has Globalization Gone Too Far?* Washington: Institute for International Economics.

Rodrik, Dani. 1998. Why Do More Open Economies Have Bigger Governments? *Journal of Political Economy* 106, no. 5: 997–1032.

Sapiro, Virginia, Steven J. Rosenstone, Warren E. Miller, and the National Election Studies. 1998. American National Election Studies, 1948–1997 [CD-ROM]. ICPSR Series 2536. Ann Arbor, MI: Inter-University Consortium for Political and Social Research.

Scheve, Kenneth F., and Matthew J. Slaughter. 2001a. *Globalization and the Perceptions of American Workers*. Washington: Institute for International Economics.

Scheve, Kenneth F., and Matthew J. Slaughter. 2001b. What Determines Individual Trade-Policy Preferences. *Journal of International Economics* 54, no. 2 (August): 267–92.

Scheve, Kenneth F., and Matthew J. Slaughter. 2001c. Labor-Market Competition and Individual Preferences over Immigration Policy. *Review of Economics and Statistics* 83, no. 1 (February): 133–45.

Scheve, Kenneth F., and Matthew J. Slaughter. 2004. Economic Insecurity and the Globalization of Production. *American Journal of Political Science* 48, no. 4 (October): 662–74.

Schmidt, Stefanie R. 1999. Long-Run Trends in Workers' Beliefs about Their Own Job Security: Evidence from the General Social Survey. *Journal of Labor Economics* 17, no. 4: S127–41.

Sinn, Hans-Werner. 2004. *Migration, Social Standards and Replacement Incomes: How to Protect Low-Income Workers in the Industrialized Countries Against the Forces of Globalization and Market Integration*. NBER Working Paper 10798. Cambridge, MA: National Bureau of Economic Research.

Smith, James P. 2003. Assimilation Across the Latino Generations. *American Economic Review* 93, no. 2 (May): 315–19.

Smith, James P., and Barry Edmonston, eds. 1997. *The New Americans: Economic, Demographic, and Fiscal Effects of Immigration*. Washington: National Academies Press.

Tichenor, Daniel. 2002. *Dividing Lines: The Politics of Immigration Control in America*. Princeton, NJ: Princeton University Press.

US Department of Homeland Security. 2004. *2003 Yearbook of Immigration Statistics*. Office of Immigration Statistics.

US Immigration and Naturalization Service. 2001. *Estimates of the Unauthorized Immigrant Population Residing in the United States: 1990 to 2000*. Office of Policy and Planning, Washington.

US Immigration and Naturalization Service. 2003. *Estimates of the Unauthorized Immigrant Population Residing in the United States: 1990 to 2000.* Office of Policy and Planning, Washington.

US Social Security Administration. 2003. Utility of Older Reinstated Wages from the Earnings Suspense File; Audit Report. Office of the Inspector General Report A-03-02-22076. Washington.

Wellisch, Dietmar, and Uwe Walz. 1998. Why Do Rich Countries Prefer Free Trade over Free Immigration? The Role of the Modern Welfare State. *European Economic Review* 42: 1595–612.

Zimmerman, Wendy, and Karen C. Tumlin. 1999. *Patchwork Policies: State Assistance for Immigrants under Welfare Reform.* Occasional Paper 21. Washington: Urban Institute.

Index

National Association of Manufacturers, 1
National Council of La Raza, 2n
National Election Studies (NES) surveys, 9, 42,
45–46
National Research Council (NRC), 38, 39, 40
national security, 1, 1n, 55
natives, 36–39, 46, 52–53, 56
compared with immigrants, 4, 8, 19–22, 20f, 22f,
28–32
naturalization rates, 30
Nebraska, 63
NES. *See* National Election Studies (NES) surveys
New Jersey, net fiscal transfers, 38–39
New York
as gateway, 5
taxation and benefits, 5
Nicaragua, 59
noncitizen residents, entitlement programs and,
13–14
North American Free Trade Agreement
(NAFTA), 6
NRC. *See* National Research Council (NRC)

occupational distribution of immigrants and
natives, 21f
occupational outcomes, earnings and, 21–22

population growth, 2
public finance, 4–5, 7, 9, 10, 27, 39–40, 41, 45,
55–56, 60. *See also* welfare benefits, welfare
participation rates, public services
public opinion, 45–46
conservative and liberal respondents, 51t
ideology and preferences, 51–52
preferences by immigrants' access to public
services, 48–51, 49t
preferences by level of education, 46–47, 47t,
48t, 49t
preferences by immigrant population, 47–48,
48t, 49t
econometric analysis of, 52
public services, 4, 9, 27
entitlement programs, US, 4
healthcare and public assistance, 28, 30n

remittances, 59
Republicans, 1, 2
residence, permanent legal, 13f. *See also* green cards
categories, 12–13

Safe, Orderly Legal Visas and Enforcement Act
(SOLVE), 58
savings and loan crisis, 6
Sierra Club, 2n
Social Security Administration, 10, 17–18, 64
cards, 17, 63
Earnings Suspense File, 17–18
Supplemental Security Income (SSI), 28, 32, 34n
Supreme Court, illegal immigrants and, 17

Tancredo, Tom, 1n
taxation, 4
benefits and, 39
illegal immigrants and, 17–18
low-wage immigrants and, 27
state income, progressive, 5, 39
tax structures and spending policies, US
states, 5
Temporary Assistance for Needy Families
(TANF), 28, 28n, 30
terrorism, 1n
Texas, 43
as gateway, 5
health services for illegal immigrants, 30n
immigration policies, 5–7
taxation and benefits, 5

union leaders, 2
United States (US), culture of, 1, 7–8
US Census Bureau, 19
US Citizenship and Immigration Services, 12.
See also Immigration and Naturalization
Service (INS)

visas
special-pool, 62
temporary, 14n, 61
temporary work, 14–15
voting, 4

wages, downward pressure on, 3
welfare benefits
availability to immigrants, 31f
welfare participation rates, 29, 29t, 35t
immigrant and native, 30f
states, 32, 33f, 34–36
welfare reform (1996), 4, 9, 29, 31–32, 53
welfare state, 1
Wilson, Pete, 5–6

Other Publications from the Institute for International Economics

DISTRIBUTORS OUTSIDE THE UNITED STATES

Australia, New Zealand,
and Papua New Guinea
D.A. Information Services
648 Whitehorse Road
Mitcham, Victoria 3132, Australia
tel: 61-3-9210-7777
fax: 61-3-9210-7788
email: service@adadirect.com.au
www.dadirect.com.au

United Kingdom and Europe
(including Russia and Turkey)
The Eurospan Group
3 Henrietta Street, Covent Garden
London WC2E 8LU England
tel: 44-20-7240-0856
fax: 44-20-7379-0609
www.eurospan.co.uk

Japan and the Republic of Korea
United Publishers Services Ltd.
1-32-5, Higashi-shinagawa,
Shinagawa-ku, Tokyo 140-0002 JAPAN
tel: 81-3-5479-7251
fax: 81-3-5479-7307
info@ups.co.jp
For trade accounts only.
Individuals will find IIE books in
leading Tokyo bookstores.

Canada
Renouf Bookstore
5369 Canotek Road, Unit 1
Ottawa, Ontario KIJ 9J3, Canada
tel: 613-745-2665
fax: 613-745-7660
www.renoufbooks.com

India, Bangladesh, Nepal, and Sri Lanka
Viva Books Pvt.
Mr. Vinod Vasishtha
4325/3, Ansari Rd.
Daryaganj, New Delhi-110002
India
tel: 91-11-327-9280
fax: 91-11-326-7224
email: vinod.viva@gndel.globalnet. ems.vsnl.
net.in

Southeast Asia (Brunei, Burma, Cambodia,
Malaysia, Indonesia,
the Philippines, Singapore, Thailand
Taiwan, and Vietnam)
APAC Publishers Services
70 Bedemeer Road #05-03
Hiap Huat House
Singapore 339940
tel: 65-684-47333
fax: 65-674-78916

Visit our Web site at:
www.iie.com
E-mail orders to:
orders@iie.com